WHERE THE DOGWOOD BLOOMS

By Elsie Cook Yelton

Edited By Carolyn Cook Davis

authorHOUSE™

1663 LIBERTY DRIVE, SUITE 200
BLOOMINGTON, INDIANA 47403
(800) 839-8640
WWW.AUTHORHOUSE.COM

First published by AuthorHouse 10/13/05

ISBN: 1-4208-8180-9 (sc)

Printed in the United States of America
Bloomington, Indiana

This book is printed on acid-free paper.

Table of Contents

Forword...vii

Introduction...ix

Chapter 1
    John...1

Chapter 2
    The Mountains...4

Chapter 3
    Little Rock Creek...6

Chapter 4
    Isabel..11

Chapter 5
    J.S...14

Chapter 6
    John's Valley..24

Chapter 7
    Ancient Times..31

Chapter 8
    The Promise...34

Chapter 9
    The Barn Raising..35

Chapter 10
    The Boraks...39

Chapter 11
    Kindred Spirits...45

Chapter 12
    Spring's Awakening..47

Chapter 13
    For Whom The Doves Mourn..49

Chapter 14

    Young George 51

Chapter 15

    Shades of Life 55

Chapter 16

    The Lost Silver Mine 59

Chapter 17

    Lost Paradise 62

Chapter 18

    The Capture 63

Chapter 19

    The Escape 70

Chapter 20

    The Homeward Journey 73

Chapter 21

    The Rebel Soldier 79

Chapter 22

    Sins Of Our Fathers 82

Chapter 23

    The Jane Bald 88

Chapter 24

    Flight of the Ravens 93

Closing Thoughts 96

Appendix A

    Little Rock Creek History 97

Appendix B

    "George Cook's Children" 98

Appendix C

    Jane's Bald on Roan Mountain 100

Index 101

Forword

Before starting this book I would like to explain to the reader why it is written in the old manner of speech that most of the early settlers used.

Had I used the modern language of today it would detract from the old time charm of the early mountain settlers, and their quaint "pleasingly odd and antique" speech which in no way reflects a lack of intelligence.

When they settled in the Toe River Valley they continued to speak the language they brought with them which many agree is Old English, not American, and many of the expressions are still used even in this modern day and age in which we live. Also, I would like to clarify that some of the words I have used are not of my choosing. One such word is "Nigger". It's just a fact of life that people used it in the old days.

It's also a fact of life that the colored race was regarded with little more compassion than the animals they worked back in the days of slavery. I have always had a deep feeling for the down trodden regardless of race or color. Men were all created equal in God's eyes and no one has the right to take another's freedom away from them.

Introduction

These characters are based on real people but naturally going back so far I have had to rely on my imagination a great deal. With all the discrepancies in the old family records, sometimes I have discarded them altogether and relied on the traditions and stories handed down from generation to generation. Some however are actual descriptions of looks and personalities. I have not even attempted to trace the family history in its entirety, it would have been an impossible task for which I have neither the time nor the inclination.

Like an old tangled ball of silk thread, I have just raveled out a strand here and there, as needed, to piece my story together.

In the crazy-quilt pattern of their lives I have sometimes discarded that ball of thread altogether. So among the silken strands, you the reader, may find a bit of yarn to give it added strength and character for the family history is like a giant jig-saw puzzle with many, many pieces missing. Lost forever in the sands of time.

At the end of some of the chapters there will be notes of explanation about people and places, so you will have a better understanding and glimpse more clearly the things I have tried to write about. The reason I gave Isabel the leading role in the first few chapters is the fact that she was my great, great grandmother and the mother of the first Cook to settle in Dogwood Flats, now known as Cook Town.

As for J.S. I am leaving it up to the reader, who can, through perseverance discover his identity. His looks and personality are figments of my own imagination. I have endeavored to be kind to my characters, over looking their seamy sides, if they had any and concentrated instead on their good qualities which far out weighs their failings.

If I seemed to write more harshly about old man Tom, it was the only way to explain my father's and Harriet's upbringing. The fact that he helped my great Aunt Judy raise nine little homeless waifs will surely tip the scales in his favor when he is weighed in the balance.

So come with me, let's take a stroll down the forgotten paths of yester-year to a world that lies buried beneath the dust of time. Where ghosts from the past still lurk, waiting to greet us if only we will take the time to dig among the debris and sift out the hidden treasures from a world that no longer exists, except in our memories.

John

Through out time immemorial men have dreamed of finding the ultimate Utopia, a place so perfect that time stands still, where there is no desire to look backward over the past or move forward into the future. More than a few in their fervor have risked life and limb, forsaking everything else dear in life in order to pursue, what for them in the end, turns out to be only a pipe dream, as elusive as a will-o-the-wisp.

On the other hand, fortune smiles on a few chosen individuals and a son of destiny, by some strange intuitive truth knows when his search is ended.

Young John, a strapping youth of only sixteen years of age stood on the brow of a high mountain, now known as the Pumpkin Patch. The beauty of the landscape almost took his breath away as he viewed it for the first time with searching eager eyes.[1]

As the scene unfolded he stood mesmerized, lost in a world where reality and fancy merged and became one. Time passed, minutes or hours, he did not know. Then the truth struck him almost like a physical blow, this was the place he had been searching for! A hidden valley closed in by high lofty mountain and suddenly a fierce feeling of possessiveness surged through his youthful heart. He had found his Shangri-La! This place was his as surely as if he had laid out a wagon load of gold bullion as its price.

Many men have found their ultimate desires fulfilled in the gold fields. Others on the high seas where they dream of finding a paradise on some uncharted island. Where life flows by like a dreamy unhurried stream. Where heart ache and worry are as distant as the stars in the Milky Way.

But whatever lay beyond the high mountains, or beneath the crust of the earth was of little concern of John's. He was interested only in the rich black soil of a land that would produce bread for his table, timber for his buildings and wood for his fires.

He wanted a place with room to breathe and freedom to roam on his own land where his future children and his children's children could sink their roots deep into the good earth and grow.

It was quite by chance that he had stumbled upon this lost world. Uninhabited and untouched by man except for the hunting trails that criss-crossed the mountains where bands of Indians and wild animals traversed.

After crossing a river, nameless at that time but now known as the North Toe, John had wondered what direction to take. As he sat on his dripping horse and as if the decision had been made for him by some strange force his horse started walking up the steep river bank. He held the reins loosely allowing him to chose the way.

The horse, a big sorrel, after ascending the river bank never hesitated. His nostrils flared in anticipation as he picked his way along the trail that followed the course of the river for some distance, then wound in and out through the thick timber in a more northerly direction.

With each clop-clop of his horse's hoofs the distant mountains, hazy and dream-like seemed to come ever closer and the voice of the wind, mournful and sobbing in the tree tops urged him on. Its wailing a reminder that a late snow storm was not impossible.

---

[1] Family records show John's date of birth as June 9, 1802.

The dead leaves and moss covering of the forest floor muted the sound of his horse's hoofs and for that fact he was grateful. He had no desire to run into a band of renegade Indians all alone in an unfamiliar territory.

As the timber thinned, he rode through an open space between two rocky, pine covered ridges with outlines as humped and crooked as the spiny backbones of two pre-historic monsters.

The sun riding clear of a ridge of stratus clouds warmed his face and he basked in the warmth and beauty of the open sky that glowed above the cloud mass, blue and serene above the uneven circle of the gray mountain rims.

Both man and beast found the brief respite from the monotony of miles beneath the veil of matted tree branches an enjoyable experience. Although devoid of foliage at that time of year, still the sun could not penetrate the gloom that cast a strange twilight effect all around them and in that shadowy world reality and fancy entwined, causing both man and horse to shy away form imagined movements behind every gnarled tree or mossy boulder.

After leaving the small open space John found himself once again being swallowed up in the denseness beneath the huge old trees that crowded the trail along a narrow valley for the next few miles, where the ancient over head branches swept so low in places he was forced to dismount and lead his horse.

As the shadows hovered like the wings of a mother bird about them he decided to make camp at the base of a mountain that loomed high against the northern sky. As he gazed at its ominous shadow he wondered what kind of dangers lay beyond its dark summit. He decided to relinquish his desire for a cheery camp fire, so with his back against a rock cliff for protection against wild animals and the cutting spring wind that howled over their heads, John and his four legged companion spent the night beneath a canopy of thick branches that ran in every direction above them and grew in every shape imaginable from the deep sloping valleys where their cattle grazed and where the family clan farmed, hunted and trapped.

John was of English descent. He had been born in Wilkes County where his fore-fathers had settled when they came to America. When he was only a small boy his father decided to leave Wilkes County to join his kin folk in the high country and although John loved his new home in the Blue Ridge Mountain and the comradeship of a large family clan, he had made up his mind at an early age to find his own mountains and valleys, away from encroachment of friend or foe where he could be master of his own destiny. A place where he could carve out a name for himself by the sweat of his face and the strength of his own two hands.[2]

As he passed through the gap in Pumpkin Patch Mountain on that long ago day near the turn of the 18th century and viewed the rugged beauty of a hidden world the future swung before him like a golden pendulum. Leaving the Indian trail and cutting across the face of the high mountain toward the west, he saw in vision a future wagon road and as he walked through the whispering yellow grass that matted the ground on the steep slope, he mapped its course in his mind.

The wind sighed in the trees along its banks and skipped and danced between the ridges and smaller hills that invaded the valley floor with their uneven patterns. Twisted old trees

---

[2] It is unclear what the date was when John first came to this area but his father Thomas Benoni Hobson was listed in Wilkes County in the 1800 census and then shows up again in 1820 in Burke County.

whose aged trunks groaned and squeaked with each blast of the cruel wind. Thick clusters of laurel with twisted branches and roots grew in tangled masses beneath the timber and served as a break from the wind for both man and horse.

Early morning found John and his faithful horse on the steep rocky face of the mountain that he had viewed with misgivings the previous evening. With his horse following close at his heels he climbed the trail that twisted its way across the face of the mountain in a north easterly direction instead of leading straight up the high summit and he soon learned the reason for the meandering trail for he came face to face to where the mountain rose on either side, to a place where a deep narrow slash in the mountain opened and was barely wide enough for a horse to pass through.

This was before man or machinery had touched the gap and the sky, like a clear blue wedge of ice, shone through the gap in the mountain. John felt a serge of excitement flow through his veins, as if he stood on the brink of a great discovery and he stopped and stood for several moments lost in reflection before passing through the gap. His horse as if understanding fully and feeling the same thrill as his master whinnied softly and lowered his head on his master's shoulder.

Stopping often to allow old Henry to snatch mouths full of the tender grass that shot up through the winter stubble, man and horse picked their way down through a steep narrow hollow to where a stream spread shallow and dandelions that bloomed along the creek-bed nodded in welcome as the soft spring breezes tousled their golden heads and the song birds flitted among the willows, their melodious cries breaking the silence of the glowing day, as if they too were welcoming him in bird language to their home among the singing mountains.

The Mountains

When John awoke the next morning the weather that had been beguiling and pleasant the day before had turned colder during the night and angry clouds scuttled over the northern rim of the mountain. He had camped higher up in the valley beside a sheltering rock with his horse tied close by. He had chosen a spot in a place that had been a water-course during the summer rains but was at present dry and sandy, where the light of his camp-fire could not be seen very far because the water course had formed a deep gash in the earth and being below the level of the land it afforded protection from the night wind and the ever present danger of Indians.

He hoped if there were Indians any where near his camp that they would be far enough away to be out of range of their being able to smell his camp-fire smoke. John had intended to let the fire die out after cooking his evening meal which consisted of wild game that was plentiful everywhere he looked, but as darkness settled down and enclosed him in with velvet softness, making the glow of his camp-fire more brighter, he became aware of glaring eyes that formed a half circle just outside the glow of the fire. "Wolves!", he thought in panic. If only he had had more time to prepare the game he had killed, cooked his supper before darkness fell and prepared his camp else where away from the scent of food. Old Henry has been restless for some time but he had laid it to the fact that the horse had not been turned loose to wallow and romp around for some time and that was his way of protesting. But the gleaming eyes outside the half circle of the firelight was proof that old Henry had been trying to warn him.

At that moment John felt very alone. To his knowledge he was the only living human soul within the black circle of the mountains that enclosed the valley and to make matters worse, at that moment a blood curdling scream split the silence. When John left his father's house he had thought only of the adventure of searching for a place that would become his future home. In his young heart he had felt he could conquer this new wilderness single-handed despite his family's dire predictions.

As the terrible scream echoed among the hills old Henry reared on his hind legs and pawed the air. It was all John could do to calm the animal who thrashed about wild eyed with nostrils flaring. John decided he would have to hobble the horse before he broke loose and bolted.

Lucky for him, there was plenty of wood within reach. The summer rains had washed the dirt from the roots of the trees and several had died during the dry spells for lack of moisture. He gathered several dry limbs and threw them on the fire. Soon he had a roaring blaze that carried dry burning leaves high into the air before falling back to earth in a powdering of gray ashes.

The sparkling jewel-like eyes had disappeared at the panther's first scream and John took advantage of the situation by breaking off larger limbs from the dead trees and piling them up for later use.

He had no time to worry about Indians at that stage. The immediate danger was the wild varmints who would close in on him as soon as the fire died down. An old stump with dry bare roots that hung down from the bank like long skeleton fingers caught John's eye. At some time high water had scooped out most of the earth and only a few strong roots held it in place but the stump was anchored more firmly in the bank than he had anticipated but he was determined to dislodge it and after much pulling, groaning and pushing the roots relinquished their hold in the soil and rolled down the embankment and landed near the fire. He proceeded to move some burning tree branches against the dry roots which soon blazed along with the limbs.

John knew the stump would hold fire until daylight with his replenishing of dry limbs now and then and that he was secure as long as he kept a blaze. John didn't bother with his bed roll that night. The heat from the fire kept him warm. Exhausted he leaned back against the sheltering rock secure in the knowledge that he was in no danger of being attacked from behind. The crackling of the fire had a soothing effect on his frazzled nerves and the big bed of live coals fascinated him as he stared into their depth and saw images among the flames as they played up and down in the heat. He saw burning mountains and burning cities that fell down and formed new images that made his eyes hurt as he gazed into their burning brightness.

Soon his fantasy faded as slumber over took the world around him but before he completely lost consciousness to his surroundings, he realized he would have to ride back to his old home, to a family clan that would be more than willing to assist him in his endeavors to make a place for himself in this lovely isolated valley between the two towering mountains.

Little Rock Creek

The men in the family clan made many trips across the wilderness trail to John's new home. They pitched in and worked like beavers during each visit. John had chosen a place near a bubbling spring to build his small cabin and on each trip after the cabin was raised they helped to get his homestead started.

Brush fences had to be built around his new grounds to keep out the deer and other animals. A two stall barn with a high sloping roof in which feed could be stored was erected for old Henry and the new cow and calf that the family had donated for John's welfare. His family had driven them across the mountains along with half a dozen sheep, a few geese and several chickens. The latter being confined in a light split-bark crate and carried on the side of one of the less stubborn pack mules.

The women folk had insisted that John needed a rooster to wake him in the mornings and hens to scratch around his barn. John found out as the first year passed that his little Eden not only flourished with every natural blessing, such as well watered land, game of all kinds-both large and small and black soil that produced corn that reached unbelievable heights but it also had its serpent that the plentiful game that always kept meat in his pot could become a curse.

Deer jumped over the brush fences and surrounded his cleared fields. Wild turkeys scratched up his grain. Dead-falls had to be set daily due to the pesky ground squirrels. Raccoons roamed at will through his corn and he had to fight for the survival of each stalk. Bears stole three of his new lambs that summer and wolves howled around his barn at night. He had to fashion a log and brush corral around the barn and drive his live-stock into it each night for their safety.

John figured when he built his cabin that it was situated far enough from the big creek so minks and weasels wouldn't be a problem. Then one morning when he went to the barn there lay five of his hens with their throats slit by weasel teeth and all their blood sucked from their bodies.

He woke at the first rooster crow and worked until the dusk of night faded objects and blended everything into blackness. Soon he found "as Adam did" that it was not good for man to live alone. He needed a family to help him if he intended to conquer this wilderness which so far had proven to be master despite all his efforts to subdue it.

Music was a gift that flowed through the family blood line. Home made banjos and fiddles hung from their walls as naturally as did the dried beans, "yarbs," garden seeds and other items that were necessary for their survival.

It was the second summer of John's abode in the section now known as Little Rock Creek and his kin folk back in the far pocket of the Blue Ridge Mountains decided it was time for the men to take the new wagon they had built for him across the mountains. So among the paraphernalia they had gathered for his comfort, carefully wrapped in separate sheep skins, a fiddle and a banjo reposed in the wagon bed. The men had expected to have a lot of labor to do and had prepared accordingly, for hither-to a wagon had never traversed the terrain. But to their surprise someone had widened the trail and wagon tracks marked the earth where only a short time before there had been only an old Indian and animal trail where horses had to be rode single file. The wagon tracks led down to the river and beyond. As the day wore on it was plain the newcomers, whoever they were, intended to stay on the trail that now angled up-ward past the last possible turn off and on toward the gap in the mountain.

A considerable amount of work had been required before a wagon and team could pass through and they wondered who had penetrated the natural barrier that led into John's private world.

As they rode across the brown of the mountain they could hear the ringing of axes and the yelling of a teamster as he dragged logs with a pair of dappled gray horses. A wagon was drawn among a cluster of trees at the base of the mountain near the creek and from the appearance of things the whole scene presented a look of permanency on behalf of the newcomers.

That night for the first time the mountains echoed the haunting strains of a fiddle, along with toe-tapping down-to-earth banjo picking. The newcomers who camped below the gap never heard the music as it floated on the dewy evening breezes, nor did they dream of the destiny that was to tie the two families together in a never ending knot of fate.

John's little pole cabin had taken on the aspect of a home instead of just a shelter from the elements and a place of safety from the wild animals that roamed the territory. Wooden spoons hung beside the wide mouthed fireplace, a wooden water bucket and gourd dipper rested beside wooden bowls on his split-log table, the legs of which were firmly driven into the ground of his dirt floor. A roll of sheep skins lay in a corner. They kept him warm as he slept during the long winter nights near the wide hearth-stones.

An iron pot, a skillet and tea kettle completed his simple cooking needs. Split baskets hung here and there on the walls, one of which was filled with many kinds of herbs, "his insurance against a bout of sickness" and their spicy fragrance filled the cabin with a homey aroma.

On this particular visit the men decided John needed a smoke house. He could smoke his meat during warm weather and keep it safe from the flies and safe from prowling varmints the year-round, so they set about the task of building one. The new structure was an odd looking little affair with a chimney reaching half-way up one wall with the mouth of the fireplace opening on the outside of the building.

After the building was completed one of the men shot a deer and even though it was too late in the season to worry about flies they hung the meat in the smoke-house and started a fire, for they liked the taste of smoked venison. The delicious scent of frying meat wafted around the cabin as the men cooked their evening meal and the big iron pot simmered in the embers of the smoke-house fireplace while mouth watering aromas ascended with the steam that billowed from around its blackened rim.

Twilight hovered, like a comforting blanket over the land, and the evening star glittered above the black rim of mountains and the late October wind moaned softly in the thick timber that surrounded the little clearing where the men had retired after supper. Stumps dotted the clearing where trees had been chopped down in order to make room for the building and one of the men strummed on the banjo they had brought across the mountains. As he sat on a big stump near the embers, while old Charley, John's dog, who lay near the embers also, watched in fascination as the foot of the banjo picker kept time with the energetic tune he had switched to as natural as if it was second nature to him. The men knew most of the old mountain ballads that were popular in that day. They were usually based on a true happening, of lovers being parted forever, or a killing, or drowning, or soldiers going off to war.

The strains of the fiddle and the lonesome words of the old songs had carried them away from their natural surroundings to a place where they felt all the pain of the happenings in the songs they sang. As if by mutual consent, the music stopped abruptly. It was time to build a roaring fire that would chase away the lonely ghosts the songs and music had conjured up.

Suddenly old Charley leapt to his feet, a sound more like a whine than a growl came from his throat as he stood stiff legged and shaking. The bristles along his back bone were standing straight and stiff. With his tail between his legs old Charley presented a very real picture of fear, mixed with a few strains of bravery as he stood his ground.

The men warned of imminent danger sprang to their feet. Too late they thought of their guns which they had left inside the cabin. Then just outside the circle of flickering light, within leaping distance, two pairs of gleaming eyes stared balefully at the little group. For several seconds no one moved and old Charley, as if frozen in stone, never uttered another sound.

Suddenly a stick of wood that had burned in two snapped and the blaze flared high in the air as it fell into the hot embers. As if by magic the glaring eyes vanished and the men and dog made a dash for the cabin. They were thankful that the sheep skins that had been trimmed and lashed together with raw hide throngs and served as a door in the beginning had been replaced with a solid door which they had split from one of the old chestnut trees that sprawled like a fallen giant at the base of a nearby hill. Hastily swinging the door shut on its leather hinges, the men made a mad scramble for their guns. Within the safety of the four walls of the cabin the men calmed down and hurriedly stirred up the embers that smoldered in the fireplace where they had cooked their supper and old Charley, shaken to the bone crawled as near to the fire as he could without getting scorched.

Meanwhile the other dogs that were tied inside the barn set to raving and howling and as they shrieked with fright old Henry stamped, snorted and pawed the walls of his stall. Luckily for the horse, they had fashioned bars across his stall door which prevented him from bolting.

The chickens, roosting on the manger were frightened out of their wits. The rooster's vocal cords, unaccustomed to so much use and strain, almost failed him. He flapped about the stall croaking hoarsely after Henry's thrashing hoofs dislodged him from his perch. Realizing the danger the cow and sheep were exposed to, trapped as they were within the brush corral, the men knew they had to do something, for the panther's screams sounded near by. Although reluctant to face the black shadows of night outside the cabin walls, never-the-less, with loaded guns and pine knots, which John had stored in the house, ablaze they ventured forth to where a big pile of brush and logs lay in a heap ready to be fired.

The log heap and brush were an accumulation from all the buildings they had raised, with the exception of the corral. The underbrush seasoned and dried flared up almost immediately at the touch of the rosin torch. With the danger of the buildings catching on fire in mind, they had piled the brush and log heap well out of the reach of the flames. They had also cleared away the near by timber, for the danger of a forest fire was ever present. As the flames rose high in the night sky the men felt a measure of safety, so they settled down on near by stumps and watched as the flames, fanned by a gentle wind carried sparks and half burned leaves into the air, where they scattered like snow flakes.

Old Charley, unwilling to turn loose of his last shred of dignity, pretended to be asleep as the men left the cabin. Nothing but his eye balls moved and in the shadowy interior of the building he had no fear of their detecting a glint from already half-closed eyes.

Isabel

A heavily loaded wagon pulled by a yoke of oxen slowly made its way along the rutted road between what is now known as Glaspie Gap and Spruce Pine. Ahead of it another wagon pulled by a pair of bay horses and equally heavy laden was driven by the head of the family clan. He was a man in his mid-sixties with gnarled hands and leathery skin made so by the many long winters he had endured along his trap lines through heavy snow, chilling rains, winds and long summers spent in the fields from sun-up till sun-down tilling the rocky rich soil on the slopes of the Blue Ridge Mountains.

As a pile of snow on the slopes of Roan Mountain clings crusty and stubborn against the first warm sun rays of spring, the old man clung to his manly strength. His eyes a deep startling blue, inherited from his mother's side of the family, still blazed with visions of a new land to conquer. His fore fathers had followed their vision, their ancestral home in England far behind them, they had climbed to the heights of the mountains and made a path for the family that he was proud to follow.

His wife, who sat on the wagon seat beside him had long since bowed to the wiles of nature. Her hair was snowy white and her skin instead of growing leathery as her husband's had done, looked waxen and tender. Her plump cheeks were lined and her lips had almost disappeared since she had lost her teeth. She had carried her years well until her youngest daughter had been born. Her complexion bathed in the fogs that settled almost daily in the hollows of the high mountains remained soft and supple as the complexions of the women in her family had once bloomed in the green countryside of old England.

After giving birth to her daughter Isabel at age fifty, the strength and vitality that had sustained her through the past years suddenly drained away and fat accumulated all over her body. Her once blonde hair became limp and thin. Not even a trace remained of the lovely woman she once had been.[3]

In her lap the family cat purred in perfect bliss as the wagon bumped along the mountain road that was still little more than a trail. Everyone in the family believed it was bad luck to take a cat or a broom when changing places of abode, so she had thrown her old broom made from a hickory sapling back on the porch of the house that had been home for so many years but she had flatly refused to leave the cat behind although she knew some of the rest of the family clan would give her food and shelter.

Now and then, Sweet Bread, for that was the cat's name, lifted a lazy eye-lid or stretched out a paw to pick happily at the material of her mistress' dress.

The other wagon was driven by a younger member of the family. They would need a strong man to get the wagons and team of oxen and horses across the river. The second wagon was loaded with barrels of shelled corn, pumpkins, potatoes, dried beans and a sack of turnips.

The wagon was packed so full a chicken crate containing an old rooster and half a dozen hens swung from the outside tied securely with raw-hide throngs. On the wagon seat beside him three guns lay in readiness. In this wild untamed country travelers had to be prepared.

---

[3] Isabel, John's younger sister was my great great grandmother.

Overhead the clouds scuttled across the November sky like a gray ghostly herd whipped by the wind that was their demon driver. Sometimes the wind dipped down over the mountains whirling dry leaves and dust in their faces causing the women who followed the wagons to bow their heads against its chilling force.

An old cow was tied to the back of the wagon and she mooed mournfully in protest. A gang of geese and turkeys were driven in front of the wagons by two boys, age nine and eleven, and Isabel, who was fourteen. The geese honked noisily as they stretched their long serpentine necks and trotted to keep ahead of the oxen. The turkeys also trotted along with the geese. The old gobbler looked and acted as if his dignity was being sorely tried as he trotted in his strutting manner, especially when the gusty wind almost turned him around in the road revealing white turnkey breast between parted turkey feathers.

Another member of the clan acted as scout. He was neither young or old, but some where in between, and a confirmed bachelor. He rode ahead of the whole procession with a big black hunting dog trotting at his horse's heels. The dog was so well trained he never made a sound without a signal from his master.

A lean old coon hound and the family dog trotted untied and assisted when they were needed with the fowl and live stock. Another man, lean and weathered as an old hickory tree, and almost as strong, led a pair of blue tick hunting dogs. His wife, broad and strong for her age walked along behind the wagons and took turns with another younger woman in carrying a ten month old baby.

No one except the family would have ever guessed the old couple in the lead wagon was the parents of fourteen year old Isabel. At sixty four her mother looked old enough to be the girl's great grandmother. If only the future could have been unveiled before the eyes of that little band of settlers who traveled that road so long ago, as it were, none of them ever dreamed the road they were traveling was destined to be one of the two main roads that lead out of the mountains. That people in the future would drive their live-stock and haul their produce down the steep winding road that is now known as Coxes Creek but at that time it was only a twisting trail traveled by Indians, for who knows how long, back in the lost past. And the other road would lead out of John's valley and across the Iron Mountain and on into Tennessee.

Gradually the clouds began to thin revealing the sky as blue as October and peaks began to appear that had not been visible before. The land was considerably smoother and more level along that stretch of road than they had been accustomed to and it seemed to the women that this surely must be the top of the world.

At a signal from the scout the little procession stopped in the middle of the road. The lead man climbed down, then assisted his wife in alighting from the wagon. At a signal from the elderly woman all the females bunched together and headed for the thicket beside the road. The dogs that were tied squatted on their haunches while the old hound and Luke, Isabel's dog, followed the women.

The men took this opportunity to cut fresh "chaws" of tobacco from the home-made twists that they carried in their pockets and motioned for the boys to take a break. The fowls stopped when the wagons stopped and one of the men went to the wagon that carried the barrels of shelled corn and scattered several hands full of grain in the road. While the geese and turkeys noisily picked up the corn the man had scattered, the men took their break by turns. It was never safe to leave wagons or a camp site unguarded. After the family had all assembled in the road again the old man lifted his head and viewed his surroundings. Virgin timber covered the ridges that rimmed the valley and in many places almost closed in the road. He had helped fell and trim many of the huge trees that lay along the road side in order to widen it so wagons could pass through more easily.

His mind, nimble as a water glider, skipped from the present back to the past winter. It had been a struggle to get the cattle fed and watered and for days he had not been able to get through the deep snows to his trap lines. Taking inventory of his situation he had made up his mind once and for all to move from his present abode and go live in the valley where his son John had settled.

His wife had already reached the point where she was no longer capable of running their home and Isabel now stood on the threshold of young womanhood. Many girls married before they had reached Isabel's age. Like a flower they bloomed and faded before reaching age twenty five due to the harsh rigors of pioneer living.

He had told the family clan of his intentions and they had given him their blessings. So between laying-by and gathering time the men crossed the mountains once more to raise a cabin near John's home so he and his family could see after them in the event Isabel should marry and leave home.

Neither Isabel nor her mother or any of the female clan had ever seen the new land where they were now headed. Isabel had longed to accompany the men folk on one of their trips. She accused them of being kinder to old Luke, the family dog, than they were to her for he had the pleasure of going on each trip they made but knowing the danger of Indians and wild varmints they had refused to take her along.

When she was told they were moving there in late fall she could hardly contain herself. She had been born after John had left home and he had children older than her. The summer had dragged by so slowly it seemed to her it would never end. Her restlessness had not gone unnoticed. She had reminded her father of John before he left home.

Soon after John had settled in his valley between the two mountains he had learned through hardship and experience that a man needed a help-mate. His need was supplied by the hand of providence. He met a girl who had come to the high country with her family on a wagon train. The courtship had been brief. After hearing about the new settlement from a member of his family who had rode in for a visit and about the good looking single girl he had seen with one of the families, he had wasted no time. The visiting relative offered to look after his things until he returned, so John had ridden through the gap never to return a single man.

J.S.

Now with teenage children and a strong healthy wife, John was destined to realize the fulfilling of his life long ambition of being a large land holder. He could now leave a large portion of the farming to his family. He was working for a man named Waightstill Avery for ten cents a day and land could be bought for five cents an acre.

He had been advised to take a large land grant. He was told if he would call it a ranch through a grant, he could obtain a thousand acres. He was also advised to bring in slave labor to work the ranch but slavery went against his grain and he didn't trust the land grants. He wanted a deed. He felt that some day when the wilderness was tamed the land would be taken back.

So with a job and cheap land available he began to save for his future dream. A few families had settled in scattered sections of Little Rock Creek and Roan Valley. Most had just settled on the place of their choice, "as John had done" without benefit of grant or deed. Since it was so sparsely settled they felt there was room for all with no fear of encroachment from their neighbors.

But John did fear that land grabbers were sure to come when the area became more settled. At the present time neighbors were a blessing, especially with the Indian situation being an ever present danger. The family clan had worried about John with so little help in the valley, especially after a man and his wife had been murdered by a band of Indians on a slope of the high mountain above the valley that later was known as Dogwood Flats. Their little son who had been playing above their cabin escaped by crawling into a big hollow log that lay on the hillside.

The old man shook his head to clear his thoughts and break his reverie. Here, miles away from the destination with women, children and live-stock was no place for wool-gathering.

Slowly he moved toward the lead wagon. His wife followed at his heels still carrying Sweet-Bread who looked a little annoyed at being aroused from her cat-nap.

Suddenly, due to November's capricious nature the blue sky was blotted out again by scurrying clouds and the wind swept down from the north ruffling goose down and causing the startled gander to honk at the top of his lungs. The old rooster, excited by the noise from the other fowls, began to cackle loudly setting off the hens that were cramped inside the crate. The worried dogs began to bark and old Luke, the family dog of uncertain ancestry, over whelmed by all the strange happenings sat down in the road and howled pitifully.

When the clamor finally stopped the old man started the team straight into the path of the gusting wind which whipped the women's long dresses about their legs and their bonnets were little protection from the grit and leaves that blew in their faces.

Isabel, the fourteen year old girl, seemed to draw from a boundless source of energy. Her cheeks glowed from exertion, cold and the excitement of the day. Her eyes, deep blue like her father's, sparkled like dew drops caught in the first sun rays of a May morning. Her dark hair touched with red highlights curled around her face where the wind had jerked it from beneath her bonnet.

Her father's hair was dead black and as straight as an Indians. She had inherited her curls from her maternal grandmother along with the red highlights. She was of average height, well rounded but slim as a sapling and as strong as a work horse. Exuberant because she was leaving the Blue Ridge Mountains forever except maybe an occasional visit back to the old home place. She had often been plagued with a smothering feeling like being buried alive for she seldom saw anyone except family and peddlers during the fall season who stopped on their way across the mountains to peddle their wares.

She had been almost overwhelmed when her parents had decided to leave the old place to younger members of the family clan and go live near their oldest son John in a section of the far mountains that was now more settled and which she knew in her heart would be wild and beautiful.

Isabel wished she could swish through the air like a witch on a broomstick and be there before night-fall. If only the oxen weren't so slow! If only they had not waited until November! But the corn had to be gathered and shucked, the potatoes dug, along with dozens of other things.

The lead wagon was stuffed with house-hold plunder, the accumulation of a life time and more, for many items had been handed down through the generations from family to family. The old wooden butter churn for instance, and the oven, and iron pots, and the trunk that was now packed with clothes and keep-sakes had once belonged to Isabel's great grandmother on her maternal side of the family.

The wagon also carried two huge feather beds and four goose down pillows, quilts pieced in different patterns, and most highly prized of all, a spinning wheel.

They came to a place where a few hundred yards ahead the road was hidden by a sharp bend. The horses and oxen had settled into a slow, steady pace and the geese and turkeys were spread out in the road trotting along very nicely now that the wind had ceased its harsh blasts. The scout had disappeared from sight after rounding the bend and the road stretched straight ahead for some distance. Reaching the end of the straight the scout left the main trial and rode through the timber and came out on the crest of a hill. An Indian trail twisted its way snake fashion across the face of the ridge below where he stood. Suddenly a lone rider dashed into view. He was mounted on a huge black horse and two black and yellow tan hunting hounds ran before the galloping horse.

The rider appeared to be as over sized as the hounds and horse and the scout up on the hill decided the size of the man, dogs and horse were a trick of the afternoon light. Then like a flash the scout thought of the family, fowls and live-stock on the road. Riding as hard as he could and hoping the rider would turn north when he hit the main trail, but alas! As he came out of the timber he saw horse and rider disappear around the steep bend heading south!

As the hounds and horse dashed around the turn in the road pandemonium broke loose. The fowls scattered in panic. Turkeys and screaming geese, senseless in their fright tried to fly over the wagons and their heavy bodies crashed into the frightened horses and oxen instead. They ran helter-skelter in every direction, flapping their wings hysterically.

The stranger's two hounds leapt aside and stood stiff legged beside the road, the bristles along the length of their back bones standing stiff. They never uttered a sound but they kept their eyes on their master's face as if waiting for a signal from him.

The rider pulled at the horse's bridle so hard he reared up and pranced around on his hind legs. The family dogs barked fiercely and the rooster got into such a dither his cackle became scrambled. The stranger's horse rolled his eyes nervously and moved around with short dainty steps like a Spanish dancer. At last the rider calmed the horse enough to slip from the saddle. He was a giant of a man and his fringed buck skin coat and tight britches gave him the appearance of having been poured into them. Thick tufts of red hair stuck out beneath his hat brim and soft looking leather boots completed his outfit. He sported a huge drooping mustache a shade lighter than his hair and contrary to his over sized appearance, his voice was soft and cultured and his manners bespoke of a more gracious kind of life than these mountains offered. His eyes, the color of bluets that bloom on fragile stems along the sides of mountain branches in early spring, held a far away dreamy quality.

"Never reckoned I'd run into arything sech as this", he said, as he swept off his hat and bowed slightly. "I wuz just letting old Caesar stretch his laigs a bit. I seldom see a family with live-stock and fowl aheadin in this here direction this late in the season. I'm mighty sorry fer scattering the fowls like at and acausing all the ruckus, not to mention almost arunnin over you folkses in the bargain!"

"Nary need to apologize", the old man in the lead wagon said. "Hit's not yer fault, but ourn, one uv my boys is up ahead to see the way wuz clear. Don't know whar he got to but like you say, we didn't expect to meet abody".

The hounds with red tongues lolling stood waiting for their master to mount. As the red faced scout came rushing around the bend they acknowledged him with a friendly wag of their tails and as the boys and Isabel moved from the place where they had stood frozen, one of the hounds reached out a drippy tongue and gave her a lick on the back of her hand.

The stranger smiled at Isabel and said "I've never knowd old Nimshi to be so taken with anyone before, him an old Samson are mighty particular fellers". With a wave of his hand he spoke to the people before him, "I'll ride old Caesar back a few paces and tie him, then I'll help git the fowls back together".

The family protested but the stranger was determined. Soon the turkey and geese were back on the road picking up corn the two boys had scattered and the incident of the past few minutes forgotten. The men gathered around the stranger explaining their plans and destination but the women stood back, shame faced, for their wind blown appearance left much to be desired.

The stranger insisted on riding along with them at least to the river crossing. His exuberant spirit proved to be contagious. Soon Isabel and the boys were singing merrily as they walked behind the geese and turkeys. Then during a pause to catch their breath the stranger started singing an old British ballad. His strong voice flowed so sweetly and smoothly that despite the clopping of the horses' and oxen's hooves, the travelers could hear every word.

> The wind doth blow today my love,
> And a few small drops of rain
> I had but one true love,
> In cold grave she is lain.
>
> I'll do as much for my true love
> As any young man may,
> I'll set and mourn all at her grave
> For a twelvemonth and a day.
>
> The twelvemonth and a day being up
> The dead began to speak
> "Oh, who sits weeping on my grave,
> And will not let me sleep".

Tis I my love, sits on your grave,
And will not let you sleep
For I crave a kiss from your clay cold lips,
And that is all I seek.

Isabel's mother had not heard any of the old British ballads for many years. They had been replaced by the younger generations with mountain ballads. When she had been a young girl growing up, her mother and grandmother had sung them as they went about their daily tasks and hearing one now on a lonely road between her dead past and uncertain future put her in a pensive mood.

Sensing the sadness he had caused by his singing the stranger suddenly touched spurs lightly to Caesar's sides and galloped ahead. Long after he had vanished from view they could hear his voice clear and melodious and some how Isabel knew the words of the songs were his own and not written verses from a book as his first song had been and the humor of them struck the girl as hilarious.

I revel in winter's cold and wind,
And summer's heat and dust.
Although I'm healthy as King George's horse,
I suffer from wander-lust.

I swim in the cold, cold mountain streams,
I climb where the eagles fly.
And if I don't fall and break my neck
I'll live until I die!

The procession journeyed on for maybe an hour. Time was hard to measure at this juncture, sometimes reality and fancy merged and without a glimpse now and then of the stranger, Isabel in her dreamy reverie could easily believe him to be a figment of her imagination but as they neared the summit of a gently rolling hill she saw him waiting beneath a tree where another Indian trail led into the main road.

"Thought I'd rest you fer a spell", he said to the old man as the lead wagon came abreast and stopped. "I'll drive the team and you can ride Caesar. The road roughens considerably frum here to the river seeing as how the heavy summer rains almost washed hit away".

The old man climbed down and motioned for the man to take his place, "I'll lead the horse, need to stretch my stiff legs a might". He walked a few yards ahead to where the hill dropped steeply below him. Laurel roots stuck out of the naked earth along the road banks posing danger to live-stock and humans alike. Heavy rocks, where the ground had softened, had slid from the banks and now lay in the road which in several places had gullies from rivulets of gushing rain water and which now lay dry and cracked like the lips of a toothless giant.

The old man felt a touch of dismay. The afternoon was waning and the wind was harsh as it sucked up the road from the river. He shook his head as if to clear his thoughts, then he grinned and said to the stranger, "Well, us men have crossed this here river afore, only once with a wagon. We'll have to do a little work on the road before going down to the water".

The stranger slapped his thigh and exclaimed, "Now I know why yer face seems familiar. I met a settler about a year ago several miles north uv here, on the top uv a mountain where a meader runs fer miles across hit's top, out near some high bluffs. His name was John and he's the spitting image uv ye, only a lot younger".

"That's my youngest boy!" the old man said. "He left home when he was only sixteen, he married between two mountains. One's the high mountain you just spoke uv and the valley where he settled is where we're heading, and which he vows someday he'll own."

"Well," the stranger said, "seems like your son has a lot of plans fer that section, a man has a right to his dreams". As he spoke the stranger lifted his eyes to where the clouds dipped and merged with the high peaks, and said as if speaking to himself, "a man can live with himself as long as he follows his dreams. When they die, he dies". The far-a-way look vanished as the old man's voice brought him back to the present, "I plumb forgot to ask your name amidst all the hustle and bustle."

In a most congenial manner the stranger said, "Jest call me J.S. That makes hit short and easy to remember." The old man stretched out his arm and with a worn paw-like hand clasped the hand of the stranger in friendship and said, "That's as good a handle as any. Well, J.S. ifen you insist on helping with the river crossing me and the boys will clear the way a mite." Soon the chips were flying and rocks were rolling. Isabel and the other women pitched in and dragged limbs from the road. After the men chopped down a large tree they notched and felled it so it would fender the steep side.

The laurel roots were next to go. Soon the way was safe for the wagons. At the river bank J.S. said to Isabel before he started the team across, "yur brother can take you across on Caesar's back. Hang on tight, the river is mighty cold!" Safe on the other side the little group assembled in the road again. The crossing had proved uneventful but a thrilling experience never-the-less for Isabel and the boys.

The dogs had to swim. They looked cold and miserable as they scrambled onto the northern bank and then there were stiffening of legs and flapping of ears as they shook off the cold river water. Old Luke headed straight for Isabel because he craved her comforting nearness in this time of need. Before she realized what was taking place old Luke stopped and stiffened his legs and lowered his head. Isabel let out a squeal as the cold water that had soaked the dog's hair sprayed her already cold feet and long skirt tail. After the first shock from the cold water wore off she smiled and shook her skirt shedding most of the water from the thick material.

After all she was not nearly as wet as old Luke who stood shivering by her side. One of the women gave her their apron to dry off her feet. her raw-hide moccasin-style shoes had also shed a lot of the water, so with the help of the apron she was soon almost as good as new!

J.S. before taking his leave told them about a likely place to spend the night, "The road is trimmed out enuf fer a wagon to git right up to the barn. Hit's on the right side of the road about half a mile offen the main trail. A settler and his family built a small cabin and barn but after awintering there they moved on. The cabin burned down last summer but the spring is running over. Drunk there myself a while back. The barn will be a shelter frum the wind."

He tipped his hat and swung into the saddle. Caesar was hot from the exertion of crossing the river, not once but three times. First with Isabel behind her brother, then the other two women. Isabel's mother had crossed in a wagon. As Caesar stood steaming like a pot J.S. said, "I'll take old Caesar across while he is still wet, then when he dries he won't have to face the water again."

After thanking J.S. for his help, they stood and watched until he forded the river again. He raised his hat high in the air in fair-well. Then the timber swallowed him from their view.

They found the barn easily enough. It was a medium size building with three stalls and a hay loft which was filled, much to their delight, with dry, fragrant hay. The spring was walled up with flat rocks and was brimming over with clear, sparkling water.

They watered the animals at the spring branch that trickled merrily through the little clearing, then vanished into the deep woods. They fed the fowls as dusk was settling beneath the timber. The clouds had thinned leaving the mountains bathed in a reddish glow. Then the turkeys and geese were driven into one of the stalls and the boys untied the raw-hide throngs and carried the crate inside where they turned the chickens loose with the turkeys and geese.

One of the women milked the cow in a wooden pail that had been stashed in one of the wagons. Then she drove her into one of the stalls and fed her shelled corn which she poured into a manger-box that was made from a part of a hollow log. The ends of the box were made from roofing shakes and fastened with wooden pegs.

The men fed the horses and oxen and their next task was getting wood for the night. A big tree stood near where the cabin had been. The flames from the burning building had scorched the bark and it stood a silent witness, like the old chimney stack, to other fires, to other gatherings.

The old man started a fire in the blackened fireplace using flint, powder and dry bark he had stripped from the inside of the peeled logs of the barn. The thin fibers of the inside layers between the logs and outside bark were almost as fine as thistle-down. They flared instantly when touched by a spark from the flint.

As the men chopped down the blackened old tree and worked it up, the women prepared for the night. Isabel and her mother had filled two bed-ticks with fresh new shredded shucks.

The opening in the center that was always left open so the shucks could be stirred, was sewed up so the shucks could not spill out. The women carried one of the bed-ticks up the ladder. One went first through the scuttle hole and stood in the barn loft, while the other two women pushed and stuffed the bed-tick through the opening. The woman in the loft pulled, and tugged with all her might. Finally the woman puffing and blowing settled the bed-tick on the hay and then they carried pillows and quilts up the ladder.

They would have to lay cross-wise in order for them to have room to sleep but in the early days families were used to sleeping scrounged up, so that didn't pose a problem.

The man who served as scout carried a big roll of sheep skins up to the loft and untied them. The men could sleep on the sheep skins which he spread out on the hay. He piled the hay higher in places so they could sleep in a kind of sitting position with the hay for a back and neck rest. The skins and their own body warmth would keep them comfortable.

The dogs were tied to the tree-laps the men had just felled to keep them out of the way. The scout had shot a wild turkey gobbler back along the way for the dog's supper. Before leaving the Blue Ridge the women had prepared food for traveling. All the hearth-stones of the family clan had glowed with hot embers in order to bake large quantities of good brown oven bread.

Isabel had made pop-corn balls. She had poured warm honey over the pop-corn and with moistened hands worked them into huge balls before the honey cooled. There were thick slices of baked ham packed in a large wooden bucket and baked potatoes, onions and best of all, there was good sweetbread.

They had no drinking vessels except a long handled gourd scoured white with ashes and sand that served as a water dipper. So why not use it for drinking the milk that foamed white and frothy in the milk pail?

It was a feast indeed for the weary travelers.

The first trip the men had taken along this route had been in early spring between planting time and the first hoeing. They had camped off the main trail to be safe from Indians and wild varmints. November was no time to travel with women folk, children and live-stock. The weather being as changeable as a woman's mind.

Lucky for them the November rains had not yet come; therefore, old Toe had flowed on neutral ground, neither friend nor enemy. He could be a formidable foe at flood-stage.

The family finally settled for the night and the man who served as scout took the night watch. Someone had to sleep with one eye open so he volunteered. Setting on a sheep skin and leaning back against a tree lap that he had chopped off for that purpose, he settled down in contentment. He loosened the old hound and Luke. Now they lay at his feet soaking up the warmth of the fire.

The stars twinkled through the puffy white clouds and the mad-caps crackled madly around the fireplace and his mind drifted from the day's happenings to light slumber. Sometime later the dogs woke him with their fierce barking. Something in the woods had disturbed them. Old Luke growled low in his throat and his neck bristles were standing stiff.

The scout got up and refurbished the fire and the flame flared high and glowing. He knew he was safe from wild varmints as long as the fire gave light but skulking Indians were a different matter. They could pick him off easily as he sat in the glow of the fire.

Apparently it had been a venturesome animal that had fled at the sound of the barking dogs for they quieted down and soon dozed again. Fully awake now, the man sat as if asleep but his mind was alert.

He knew he was different natured from the rest of the men in the family clan. He had left home one time and had been gone for two long years. He had longed to see what lay below the Blue Ridge Mountains. On that journey he saw many things that amazed and mystified him. He also saw may things he didn't like: slavery was a raw evil that stuck in his craw and stayed there.

He had met other fellow travelers on the road of life and heard many strange tales as they sheltered beneath a bridge or camped in the open beside a campfire. He had heard of their dreams and their failures. One old man in particular had caught his attention more than the others as he talked of the sea as if it was a living thing.

The old man had a way of making his stories come alive in a fashion that conjured up visions of blazing sunsets that turned the water into an ocean of blood. He spoke with deep reverence as he painted scenes as vivid with words as an artist could paint with his brush.

After hearing the old man's tales of the sea and its mysteries, he knew he would never stop his journey until he had viewed if for himself. When at last he had stood on a sandy beach and had watched as the green waves washed upon the shore, he had felt an over powering sense of his smallness.

The beauty of the whole expanse of the water and the waves that tossed like a living thing trying to escape their bounds gave him a heady feeling. He felt like he had just tasted a rare wine but it was much more lasting for it was something he could re-live over and over when the actual scenes around him were stark and lonely.

He was blessed with a gift that few people possess. Like drinking a nectar of the Gods and reaching an all time high while he himself faded into insignificance before one of the great works of the creator. It was at that moment in his life as he gazed out over the ocean whose agonized restlessness struck a cord from somewhere deep within his being that a truth bubbled up to the surface of his consciousness that he had never realized before. Now he knew if he, like the old man, could paint scenes with words about places and things, it would have to be about the valleys and mountains. Despite all its beauty he could not picture a world of water and storms and all the dangers of the deep and he realized a man had to be borne to a certain kind of life before he could love it as the old man loved the sea.

As he stood there that day with his feet buried in the sand, he recognized the feeling that had been gnawing at his insides for what it was. He had reached his journey's end and he was terribly home-sick for the mountains and kin-folk.

He closed his eyes and saw in a vision the lofty peaks of his birthplace. Blue green mountains with the summer heat dancing on Elfin feet against their rugged slopes, then like magic he could see autumn shades stretched like purple patches sewn with scarlet threads across their encircling expanse. Facing homeward again he had traveled more slowly taking in the sights of the low country, working in exchange for a home cooked meal and living off the game of the land when he could not find work.

On the last lapse of his wanderings before starting the ascent of the mountains he had chanced upon a boarding house. He stopped and asked for work in exchange for a meal and a night's lodging.

The owner's wife ran the place. Her husband was crippled and it so happened she had a lot of work that needed to be done. During the course of the evening his host told him how the boarding house had come into existence. After her husband's accident neighbors and kin-folk alike had offered to help in any way they could, so she had told them if they really wanted to help, they could do so by building her another room. She felt she could support her family if she had more room, so they built, under her instructions, a large room that spanned the length of her two rooms and a porch of equal length plus a wide fireplace.

They were situated near the trail that led out of the mountains, so she fed travelers and put them up for the night.

She also raised vegetables and kept a cow. She made the kitchen her family room and the other room was where she bedded down her boarders. The new room served as a living and dining room. Her boarders could set before the fire and talk until bed-time which was as soon as the work was done and the kitchen cleaned.

His first day at the boarding house proved to be a busy one. He had chopped and stacked a mountain of wood, he had repaired the old worm fence around her garden and cleaned out the barn.

The woman worked long hard hours and she expected him to do the same but one thing he could say about her, the lady sure could cook and the bed she put him in was something he had dreamed about on nights when he had tried to sleep on the hard ground with only his horse and pesky insects for company.

He spent three days and nights at the boarding house. Never had he seen so much work to be do at one place and never had he faired so well. Maybe he had a hungry look about him that appealed to the woman or maybe it was his willingness to work that made her feel she had to feed him so much. Whatever the reason, he soon began to feel like a stuffed turkey and it was a joyous feeling after long months of feeling empty most of the time.

On his last night at the boarding house a peddler that he was acquainted with stopped to spend the night. The peddler had spent several nights at his parents house as he traveled with his horse and pack mule across the Blue Ridge. After supper they had struck up a game of chance but he had nothing to bet on but a pocket knife and his horse, which he needed. The peddler was set on playing because he was a born gambler and often returned to the mountains poorer than when he left.

Earlier that day the peddler had traded several household items to the inn-keeper's wife for a spinning wheel because the woman said she was too busy to use it now that she had the boarding house to run.

He had thought of his mother and how pleased she would be if he could win the spinning wheel for her and so in a reckless moment he had bet his horse against the spinning wheel and to his amazement had won. It has been in the bargain for the peddler to deliver the spinning wheel to his home, so after dismantling it and tying the wheel to the pack mule's back, they started for home.

The peddler reassembled it for his mother and she used it with great pride. In the following years it became the family's most cherished possession and was dismantled and moved to John's valley with their other wares.[4]

Upon his return to his parents home, he had settled into the daily routine of chores and his home sickness for the mountains and his kin-folks was cured. After a short period of time his mind began to wander back to the ocean and to other places that he had seen in his travels.

Now as the sat beneath the open bowl of the sky other dreams were forming. He had hesitated to leave home again feeling his parents needed him. Now they were going to live near his younger brother John who would look after them and he could make plans of his own. Deep down in his heart he knew his father didn't trust his restless nature and that was the reason for his moving to John's valley. John had always known exactly what he wanted out of life, while he, like the troubled waves of the ocean, never knew what strange paths his feet would find.[5]

---

[4] There are still parts of an old spinning wheel that once belonged to my great Aunt Judith "Judy" as she was lovingly remembered. My father often talked of how she worked to feed and clothe the nine children she had undertaken to raise. She would set and spin by the firelight and a small tallow candle that flickered on the mantle. The spinning wheel had been handed down through the generations and was worth it's weight in gold for home spun clothing was what most of the early settlers wore in this mountain section.

[5] There is evidence that a branch of the Hopson family really did migrate to the west and settled there. Nellie (Mrs. Baxter Hopson) the oldest survivor on the Cook side of the family, (she was Jane's granddaughter) told me about two men by the name of Mose and Mark Hopson who came to their house from California searching for their family roots. She filled them in on the family history as

Nodding by the warm fire beneath the limited view of the blue November heaven, hemmed in on every side by looming dark mountains, his day dreams slipped into quite slumber as the fire burned low in the smoke blackened fireplace and the moaning night wind went unheard in the little clearing.

---

best as she could, then sent them to John Hopson's granddaughter, Bessie (Mrs. Hobert Ledford) the oldest survivor on the Hopson side of the family.

I talked with Bessie about the visitors from California, she said she filled them in on what she knew of the family history, she said they wanted to talk with Bessie's father Joseph Hopson because he was the oldest member of the family at that time but Joseph was sick and in the Banner Elk hospital. Due to the seriousness of his illness "which proved to be his death-bed sickness" Bessie refused to tell them of his whereabouts.

Mark and Mose told their Little Rock Creek relatives that one of their ancestors had struck it rich in the gold mines. Apparently, no one wrote down Mark and Mose's parents names and if they left their address by the time I talked with Nellie and Bessie it has been long forgotten and that branch of the Hopson family has never been heard from again.

John's Valley

The wind moaned softly as it passed over their heads. At times it shrieked and howled on the high ridges but the little group of people paid scant attention. They were on their way again and in high spirits.

The scout walked ahead up the steep grade with his horse following at his heels. He was determined never to have the fowls scattered again. He kept an alert eye on the surroundings. Huge old trees grew along the road sides and gray squirrels played among them showing little fear.

The dogs that were loose darted in and out of the timber and the distasteful scent of a skunk permeated the air. "Ifen one uv em rascals gits sprayed I declare I'll hang him!" one of the women said. As she sniffed the air, "That stuff always gives me a headache every time I smell hit."

The two dogs came back to the road and as luck should have it neither one had the scent on them. They acted kind of sneaky and stayed close to the wagons. The scout thought back over the ground they had covered that morning. For several miles it had been comparatively the same, then gradually the grade had steepened. Now they found themselves ascending a steep mountain side and the twisting road was treacherous and narrow. Steep rugged mountains rose up to the far right with smaller razor backed ridges in between and pines and scrub oak grew along their spines.

Below the road they could see a deep narrow valley. If one of the wagons should tip over, the valley would be its splintery grave. Suddenly, on their left they could see the northern skyline through the trees and Isabel knew they were near the summit.

The mountain at that point seemed to close in on either side. It loomed high and dangerous looking to her as she gazed through the trees that were silhouetted against the sky. Then after turning a stiff bend in the road they saw ahead a gap in the mountain. It looked as if a giant hand had reached down some time in the eons of lost time and had jerked the mountain apart.

The women had not been told about the gap. The men had talked it over and had decided to let them discover things for themselves. Isabel forgot about the geese and turkeys. She rushed ahead to where her brother was waiting.

The drivers drove the team and oxen to the left and stopped after passing through the gap and the family all gathered on the brow of the mountain and looked with wonder at the splendor that unfolded before them.

Isabel stood enraptured after crossing the river the previous day. They had glimpsed from time to time a circular mountain with a forked formation on what seemed from that view its western shoulder but standing near the gap now, they could see the other half of the mountain and the strange rock formation was directly north.

The mountain sat like a huge brown hen with the lesser mountains sticking out beneath her wings like baby chicks. The Fork Mountain bluff her head, the rocky face of the cliff below the bluff her breast and the white streaks pinkish now from the sinking sun her speckled feathers.

The streaks of white were huge old chestnut trees that had died there on the mountain. Most of them a natural death but some of them had been struck by lightening. Their giant limbs stretched toward the sky bare of bark and bleached white like huge prehistoric bones by the weather. They had witnessed more passing time than any human being could ever hope to witness.

No one in the little group on that long ago day ever dreamed those huge giants were doomed to vanish forever from the mountains, killed by the plague of the blight.

The sky this day was not so heavily laden with clouds as the preceding one had been. A pale blue sky touched with hues of pink was prevailing. Scattered clouds white and fluffy sailed over the northern mountains casting dark shadows on their slopes.

The old man's eyes dropped from their wanderings to Isabel's face where emotions played like the light and shadows on the steep ridges and for a moment his mind went back to his lost yesterdays to another daughter. His first born, whose nature had been as gentle and warm as a spring day, who had blended into everyday life so perfectly and was so much her mother's daughter. He had never had to correct her in any way. A daughter who had married at age fifteen and died at twenty five leaving five orphaned children behind.

Isabel tore her eyes away from the distant mountains and focused them on her nearer surroundings. To the left a meadow fell steeply at their feet, sloping all the way down to a creek whose waters reflected the sky like a molten looking glass.

The east was rimmed by a steep rugged mountain. Green spots dotted its rocky face where laurel patches grew thick and matted. An Indian trail hugged the base of the mountain from the gap all the way to the creek where a giant tree had been felled providing a crossing place.

Isabel saw that in order to get a wagon across the stream the road to the left had to be used. It cut across the face of the high mountain on which they were standing, then turned steeply downward to where the creek spread broad and shallow over the sand and rocks.

This ford of the creek, the men knew, would soon be frozen solid so wagons and teams could cross without breaking the ice. No one spoke or moved out of their tracks for an indeterminable amount of time as if frozen in stone. The wind whined softly like the voice of a wolf whelp on the high peak behind them. Across the creek a valley ran from east to west with encroaching foothills and ridges.

Isabel was glad the timber had shed its foliage so she could get a better view of the lay of the land. She drank in the whole scene before her from the top of the highest mountain to the valley floor. Now she knew why her brother had chosen this place for his home and from this day forward it would be her home too. This beautiful land of promise would never make her feel smothered as the home behind her had. Here she could breathe and be free.

At last, roused from their reverie, the family reluctantly took their places in the road again. Old Luke stuck close to Isabel's heels while watching the fowls all the while and keeping them in line.

The foot-bridge over the creek was a curiosity to Isabel. She had always crossed streams on fallen logs. Sometimes they were hewn flat on top for more sure footing or on rocks when the water was down. It was plain to see the bridge had required a lot of thought and patience. Two logs, long and strong, but not so very large in circumference spanned the creek. Short lengths of logs about the same size of the supporting ones were notched cabin fashion and fit down over the foundation logs. They were not laid solid but spaced about a normal step apart. The rains and dampness of the creek had swollen the logs and they were locked together as firmly as if they had been pegged down.

Isabel and the boys skipped across the foot-bridge and the dogs followed. After crossing Isabel skipped half-way back again. The foot-bridge was high over the water in order to prevent it from washing away during the heavy summer rains and there were no hand rails.

Below the ford a large rock stuck up on the creek bank. On the other side several smaller rocks were piled together until they were equal in height to the big rock. The supporting logs of the bridge rested on these two foundations.

Stepping stones led up to the rock footing. Isabel sat down in the middle of the bridge and let her legs gangle over the edge, then lying down full length, she peered between the logs. The moving water made her head swim and she felt as if she were floating away, weightless as a feather.

Come on Aunt Isabel, the boys urged, "Let's git the geese and turkeys agoin." At the sound of their voices she rose from the bridge, careful of her footing until her head cleared. They came up from the creek to where the road merged with the main road that led in and out of the valley and turned east.

Over in the field that ran from the gap to the creek they could see a settler's cabin smoke curling up from the chimney only to be carried by the wind against the mountain from whence they had so shortly descended, where it banked, thin and misty looking. Several people stood in the yard, shading their eyes with their hands against the late sun rays. They watched until the wagons were out of sight.

A short distance up the road on the left Isabel could see a big, almost level, open field. The road embankment blocked her view to a certain extent but she could tell by the corn stalks the field had been tended the past summer. At the end of the corn field she could see the Indian trail leading down from the gap in the mountain and the big tree lying sprawled across the creek, its top side almost clear of branches and the bottom side still bushy with large limbs that spread out in the water supporting and elevating the immense weight of the trunk.

The tree has probably fallen straight across the stream but now lay at an angle, swept gradually down stream by high waters and came several feet short of the northern bank. Isabel knew she could clear in one giant leap the remaining distance.

At this point where the Indian trail led up the steep embankment the road took a stiff turn. As they rounded the bend, the high shoulder of the ridge above the road cut off the last rays of the dying sun and the straight stretch in the road ahead lay in deep shadow.

Large trees grew along the roadside. Through the timber on the right she could see the creek flowing widely over rocks, some of whom were barely below the surface. The water sheeting like glass as it moved slowly along its way to meet the river.

On the opposite side of the water a streak of dying sun, unblocked by the high ridge, lighted the terrain in a strange and unnatural glow, etching in sharp detail the evergreen laurel leaves in a thicket that covered the face of the ground giving the gray trees that stuck up above the green tangle a pinkish red color.

At the sound of a shout Isabel turned her gaze from the rugged scenery and saw near the end of the straight a cabin nestled above the road and a man hurrying along with a child in his arms, followed by a woman who was waving her arms in greeting.

It was her brother John and his wife Elizabeth. Shouts rose from the group behind her and old Luke dashed ahead yapping joyously and greeted John with a flying leap. A girl, taller than Isabel and two slender young men came running to meet them, while a child of four years or so tried to keep up with them on his chubby short legs.

Isabel rejoiced in the fact she had reached her destination. She left the geese and turkeys to trot unattended and hurried ahead with the two boys to meet them in the early gloaming.

Isabel woke at the first cock crow. The cabin was shrouded in blankets of darkness and her parents snoring sounded like a ghostly duet. Lulled by the seemingly unearthly sounds she drifted from time to time back into the land of dreams but the faithful old rooster brought her back to reality each time.

Finally, unwilling to take the chance of falling into deep sleep, she crept quietly from beneath the covers, careful not to wake the sleeping children who had shared her bed and dressed in the soft blackness.

She had dressed all her life in this manner, more by sense of touch than of light. The glow from a fireplace seldom flickered to the back end of a cabin where the beds always were placed.

Feeling her way noiselessly to the door, she slipped outside and was engulfed in velvety shades of darkness almost as black as the interior of the cabin. Isabel stood still in the inky denseness for a few minutes trying to get her bearings. Not even one single object could be discerned. Finally she groped along until she found a porch post. Standing there all alone in the crisp pre-dawn air, she lifted her face to the sky and not even a star lighted the whole heaven. It was merged with the mountains into one solid mass of blackness.

Gradually the eastern sky lightened and the clouds began to vanish as if by magic leaving the rim of mountains etched in stark outline. Something soft and cold touched her hand and a whine barely audible told her old Luke was ready for the new day also.

As daylight crept over the earth enough for her to see her way clearly Isabel headed for the creek. Being endowed with a healthy curiosity and a daring nature, the big tree that lay in the water was a challenge. It was safe enough, the springy limbs that supported it being many and strong.

The main problem was balance but the danger of falling off the wobbly log only enhanced the adventure. She squatted in the sand beside the cabin measuring in her mind the distance between the creek bank and the log. She felt confident she could clear the space with ease but the landing was another matter. Her long skirt would hamper her leap.

Isabel stood up and looked in all directions. The morning shadows were so deep at this early morning hour she felt confident no one would see her, so she slipped out of the cumbersome garment and rolled her moccasins up in the thick folds. Then she tied it around her waist with a piece of raw-hide string. Then taking a few quick steps backward and flinging out her arms. Looking like some kind of fall bug in her long bloomers, she sailed through the air and landed on the log.

Up and down, up and down went the log, as the tree branches bent with the impact of her weight, while the rippling water beneath her moved in another direction. Grabbing a limb that stuck up near by, Isabel hung on for dear life. She closed her eyes against the moving water and the springy motion of the log until she steadied herself.

Elated, she pranced lightly over the fallen tree, then sprang onto the opposite bank where old Luke was waiting. He had acted more sensible by swimming the creek instead of clambering over the bobbing log.

Blithesome as a wood nymph, she headed up the trail that led to the gap. A brisk wind whipped across the face of the mountain. Its cold gushiness against her half dressed body sent chills crawling up her spine. Hurriedly she untied the raw-hide string from around her waist and dawned her heavy skirt. Its long thick folds were sheer delight to her chill bumpy body and legs.

She raced up the side of the ridge with old Luke at her heels, her breath a thin frosty veil of mist in the cold air. When she reached the gap, all out of breath, the cutting wind had ceased. The exertion had warmed her from head to toe and her heart pounded like a sledge hammer within her rib cage. As she stopped to take a "breather" she surveyed the upper slopes above the road she had traversed only yesterday. To her delight she saw a rock jutting out from the hillside. Its flat top surface and tapered end that seemed to rear in the air due to the slant of the land reminded her of a giant snake's head emerging from the earth.

She climbed the steep grade as graceful as a mountain cat and rested on the face of the rock between the places she imagined the serpent's eyes would be. After wrapping her legs in the folds of her skirt and padding the cold rock beneath her with the remaining material, she hugged her arms around her knees with clasped fingers, then proceeded to view her kingdom at leisure.

From her lofty perch the valley below Pumpkin Patch Mountain slumbered in deep shadows like a deep bowl of misty liquid. Isabel drank in the beauty of the landscape never dreaming she was destined to be the beginning of future generations who would live among the high hollows that now were only smudges of black in the early light.

Even though the sun was still on his upward climb behind the eastern mountains, a streak of gold flashed across the eastern half of the high rainbow shaped mountain that rimmed the valley to the north and lodged in fiery splendor against the rugged face of the Fork Mountain bluff.

Isabel gazed entranced as a cloud of fog, white as snow, drifted down over Roan Mountain and suddenly as if by magic the steep slope she had thought to be a solid mass of earth and stone seemed to split apart as the fog drifted down.

A rugged cliff suddenly took shape against the fog bank with huge pine trees growing along its top silhouetted against the white background. In later years the cliff would be known as the wildcat rock because it was the last refuge for the panthers that dened there after man began to tame the territory.

Few people ever experience the deep joy Isabel felt that morning. It seemed as if in some strange way she had become one with the universe, as if she had touched a spiritual realm beyond human understanding. She felt washed and clean as if she had been dipped into some strange and magical stream.

Trance-like Isabel rose and stared back down the narrow trail. She had viewed the mountains as the later afternoon sun had painted their rugged heights, now she had seen them while they still wore their robes of morning mists. She had visualized invisible hands smoothing out the deeper streaks of red in the eastern sky and blending them together into one smooth shade of blushing gold.

She was deeply satisfied with her morning excursion but it was time for her to help the family with the morning chores. When she reached the creek again she went through the previous motions of removing her skirt and moccasins. With arms spread like the wings of a buzzard, so she could balance herself, she walked slowly over the log and old Luke, feeling more daring, followed at her heels.

Reaching the small end of the log she sprang, bull-frog fashion and landed clear of the water. Old Luke stopped and looked at her as he neared the end of the log. She snapped her fingers and called for him to follow and with mince steps he managed to get down into the shallow water and wade out to where she waited for him.

Ancient Times

When Isabel entered the house it was astir with activity. The women were preparing the food for breakfast and the smell of baking bread and frying meat permeated the air and made her mouth water. The old kettle sang merrily on its seat in the embers.

No one asked questions about her where abouts. Her mother had given up long ago trying to understand her daughter's strange habits. She sauntered around keeping out of the way of the busy women. There was nothing she could do at the present time, even the water bucket was full, so she leaned against the door that swung on leather hinges and took stock of her brother's cabin.

It was a typical early settler's building with walls of unhewn logs with no thought of any thing but comfort. The walls were chinked with red clay mud which had dried to a brick like hardness and the dirt floor was hard packed and clean. A split broom made from a hickory sapling hung from a wooden peg on the wall.

The wide fireplace was a heap of flat stones laid with the utmost precision and daubed like the walls with clay. Wide hearthstones were placed close together before the fire-pit where the family cooking was done.

A wide assortment of barks and herbs hung from the joists. Angelica roots, dried cat-nip, penny royal, butter fly roots, gin-sang and many others too numerous to mention. Next year's seeds also swung from the joists, safe from prowling mice and two guns lay in the rack made from a forked tree limb. The rack was fastened to the wall with wooden pegs. A fiddle and banjo also hung from wooden pegs on the wall near the gun-rack. Between a bed and the front door several small wooden barrels lined up against the wall and Isabel felt sure they were filled with dried chestnuts.

One of the women called for Isabel to round up the men for breakfast was ready. At her first call everybody headed for the door but she shooed the youngsters back for there would have to be two table settings due to the large number of people. After taking a last hungry look at the big heaping wooden platter of golden pone bread that had come straight from the oven and now steamed in the center of the table, she joined them in the yard where they romped and played and tried to forget their ravenous appetite.

Finally, after a seemingly indeterminable amount of time of eating and discussing the day ahead, the men emerged from the house and all the youngsters made a mad dash for the door.

Isabel heaped her pewter plate with the delicious food because her early morning jaunt had made her more hungry than usual. The older women settled down to a more leisurely meal while all the other youngsters like Isabel wasted no time in formalities.

As she ate, out of the corner of her eye Isabel studied her oldest niece. She was slender, tall and good looking in a sinister kind of way. She had a "syrupy" way of talking and calling everyone honey but her eyes black as a midnight pool reflected no warmth and belied her sugary words. Finally, after breakfast was over and the morning chores were done, Isabel slipped away from the house. The men were in the garden digging holes to bury the potatoes and other vegetables they had brought in the wagons. The boys were off somewhere on an adventure all their own and if time had not been so fleeting she would have explored the barn first and rolled in the hay just for the sheer joy of being alive, as it was, she decided to save that for a rainy day.

She headed westward through a grove of large timber, huge old chestnut trees being the most dominant, some of whom had hollows large enough for several people her size to shelter in.

A spring branch trickled through the undergrowth and she followed it to its source where it bubbled up clear and cold beneath a cupped rock. After lying full length on the spongy earth and drinking, she struck a meandering trail through the woods where giant oaks, sugar trees and maples grouped together like sentinels guarding secrets from a lost world.

Squirrels scolded as she passed beneath the low hanging branches and as she came out into the big corn field above the road a trio of deer bounded across the field and disappeared from view through the timber. As she followed the corn rows through the field, she saw sticking up among the corn stalks dozens and dozens of arrow heads. The field looked as if it had been cleared forever since no rotting stumps were in evidence and she wondered who had cleared it so long ago.

Isabel walked the length of the field idly picking up arrow heads and the ground beneath her feet making little crunchy sounds at each step. Near the western edge of the field bushes grew in small clumps and a creek, not nearly as large as the one they had forded the day before, flowed frothy over the rocks.

Across the creek a laurel thicket grew dense. It crowded so close to the water no human could crawl through their matted branches and roots. A wide cleared place led out to the very edge of the creek and broken pottery lay scattered everywhere along the stream's edge.

Isabel leaned against a big rock that rose up from the cold depths of the water and closed her eyes because she felt light headed and faintly. The events of the past few days had been so overwhelming she felt her body was too small to contain the thrill of it all.

Unaware of the arrow heads she still held in her hands, she felt time slip backward into a world so real it was more vision than dream. Before her in the big open field an Indian village sprawled, Indian maidens, slender as willow boughs swayed with their long hair flowing, carrying water from the creek. Old squaws, wrinkled and brown, worked in the open and she smelled the smoke from their cooking fires.

She saw Indian children happy, laughing and playing at their games, then she glimpsed a slender form and watched as it glided along the creek bank, dressed in beaded white doeskin. Then suddenly there was only a face, young and beautiful with sparkling eyes, white even teeth, and skin as flawless as a rose petal.

A tiny scar, lighter in color, showed below the hairline and in a strange way enhanced the lovely features. Then the face receded into nothingness and she heard the death chant, mournful and heart rending as the whole village mourned for their fallen warriors or were they mourning for themselves as a doomed race?

Isabel heard a dog bark as plain as day and when a wet tongue touched her hand she smothered a scream and opened her eyes to find old Luke squatted on his haunches and looking up at her face in a puzzled kind of way.

How long had the dog been there? She looked down at her hands that felt stiff and cramped from holding them in the same position for how long? Time could not be measured in minutes and seconds and it seemed she had spent hours, even days, in the last few minutes.

She turned dreamily and retraced her steps through the field, stopping now and then to view the gap through which she had passed only yesterday. She wondered vaguely about the family who lived in the field below the gap but the thought soon vanished because her mind kept flitting around like the thin clouds that spread over the mountains.

Later, when Isabel asked her father's opinion on the matter of an Indian village having once existed on the big field, after pondering her question over in his mind for a while, he said, "Ain't supposed to uv ever been Indian villages in this here section. Hit's been said they only used hit fer hunt-un and battles, but seems to me thar's a lot uv evidence to the contrary".[6]

There was not a doubt in Isabel's mind. She knew in her heart an Indian village had once stood in the big almost level field that later took on the name of a bottom and that young maidens and old squaws had carried water from the creek.

---

[6] Although history disputes the fact that Indian villages ever existed in this section, old timers had their legends never-the-less that have been handed down from generation to generation.

One of the legends is about the Indian village that once existed in the bottom field near Little Rock Creek bridge.

Baxter Hopson was one of the heirs of the John Hopson property, inherited from his father Thomas Nora Hopson and even though the land has passed on to new heirs the property still bears Baxter's name.

The Promise

The next day the men hitched up the team of horses and oxen for they were going to haul wood. The women stayed in the house and cooked for the large crew and tended to the small children.

Isabel and her niece went along with the men and boys. There was a lot of laughing and singing from the youngsters as the big chips flew. It was their job to load the wagons. The men had to handle the big back logs, which once fired would last and last and when they were finally consumed into big embers they served another purpose on the hearthstones to bake the good oven bread the family was so fond of.

By the time the evening shadows gathered in the valley huge ricks of firewood were stacked near the cabin where Isabel and her parents would spend the winter. John already had his winter's supply hauled and stacked.

The women had the milking and feeding done and supper cooked by the time the last wagon load lay neatly stacked. The women swept the wagon floor after the men removed the wagon bed, then everyone pitched in and helped carry the food outside where they used the wagon for a table. In that fashion everyone could eat at the same time after filling their plates and setting on stumps and turned up cuts of firewood.

It was a delightful time for all. After the wagon was cleared and the dished washed, a big bon-fire was lit and the family danced and sang around its mellow glow.

Soon the mountain rims were as black as ebony as night settled beneath their protecting circle. This would be the last family gathering until spring when the men returned to build John's new house. By that time the earth would have shed its brown covering and donned its pastel colors of light green and pale yellow mixed with the flowering of the white dogwood and sarvis and many other shades that never failed to delight the eyes of the beholder. Finally the merry making stopped and Isabel put her arms around her two nephews. They had never been separated before and she tried to close her mind to the fact of how she would miss them.

The youngest, with big soulful eyes, looked up at her sadly and said, "I'll miss you Aunt Isabel." She hugged him and said in a comforting tone, although she felt like bawling like a young calf, "This winter will pass afore you know hit. When the men come back in the spring to build John's new house, you can come back with em to stay. Even ifen you have to sleep in the hay loft! I'll have them add a lean-to to our house so you boys will have a place to sleep."

A smile broke across the boy's face as bright as the first break of morning sun across the rainbow shaped mountain. "We'll have a good time next summer won't we, Aunt Isabel?" Then he scampered away happy as a lark.

She took her oldest nephew's hand in hers and said, " You boys be good this winter. We would keep you here ifen we could but John's house is bursting at the seams with younguns and our little place will be scrounged something awful with all our household plunder but with the coming uv spring thangs will be difrent."

The Barn Raising

Early one morning in late March the family prepared to go to the Cook's, who lived in the field below the gap, to a barn raising.

Isabel's parents were taking the wagon because her mother was short winded after being house bound all winter and several pounds heavier than she had been when they arrived at John's home in November. The women had cooked and baked in preparation for the event. A barn raising was a day of work and pleasure combined. Each family attending brought food which was served outside if the weather permitted.

Like the old saying, March comes in like a lion and consequently snow still lay on the high slopes of the mountains, tell-tale tracks of the lion but on this day in the valleys it was the time of the lamb.

Dandelions nodded golden heads like tiny suns and violets bloomed in splendor along the branches and swamps and bluets opened their eyes scathingly. Soon the warm sun would bring masses of the fragile little blue eyed flowers Isabel loved so much.

Winter had passed like a dream. After the late November rains the snow had settled down thick and cold, as if intending to stay forever and everything outside wore thick blankets of white.

As of now Isabel had not met any of their neighbors because there had been no common ground on which to meet until now. The men of the family were speaking acquaintances with men of the Cook family. They had hunted together occasionally and swapped work but that was before she had arrived in the valley.

Isabel had accompanied her father and brother John and John's two oldest boys as they set their trap lines. She had wadded deep snow with them on their return rounds. She was not squeamish because she lived in a time when women had to be strong but she always turned her face away when the killings took place along the trap lines.

She helped skin and stretch the pelts after the animals were dead. She had seen panther tracks and heard them screaming up on the high ridges. She had heard the wolves howling and seen signs of their kills in the bloody snow.

Now signs of spring were everywhere and she could hardly wait until the earth and water warmed again. She had already found a private place in the little creek where laurel grew thick on both banks. She intended to take a bath everyday when the water got a little warmer.

She knew it would never be really warm all summer long for it flowed from high up in the mountains where her father said it went underground beneath the Fork Mountain bluff but Isabel didn't care if it was chilly. Her mother would consider her completely insane if she ever found out she bathed in cold creek water but what her mother didn't know wouldn't hurt her.

Little did she dream that some day that cold mountain stream would bear the name of Cook Creek in honor of her first born son.

All the rest of the family went with the wagon except John's oldest daughter who stayed home to look after the younger children and Isabel who took the path through the timber and crossed the big field. On the far side of the field she paused to catch her breath. The early sun had already warmed the chill from the air, the silvery catkins on the pussy willows sprouted velvety from naked limbs and birds flitted among the clumps of bushes seeking branches on which to build their future nests. Isabel longed to stay where she was unwilling to miss even one of nature's glad offerings. It was with reluctance that she turned and hurried down toward the road where she trotted briskly until she caught up with the family wagon.

Men were already at work on the barn when they arrived. As the women entered the well built hewn popular log house Isabel suddenly felt shy but as they were warmly greeted and introduced she lost most of her self consciousness and began to enjoy herself. An old lady who had been presented simply as Granny Cook sat near the hearthstone and eyed Isabel with keen curiosity. A habit cultivated by most old people when they are no longer active.

A pretty young girl about Isabel's age named Lizzie Beth took her arm and whispered under her breath, "Let's go out and watch the barn raisin." Lizzie Beth was plump and blonde with creamy skin and big blue eyes. She had a bunch of violets, which were showing signs of wilting, tucked in her hair with their long stems caught beneath her heavy braids.

The girl giggled and blushed as they passed a dark haired young man who was straining with all his might at a log he and another young man about the same age were trying to lift. Isabel saw Lizzie Beth and the dark haired young man's eyes meet for a fleeting moment but it was enough to tell her the two were lovers.

Isabel felt her cheeks flush as she looked into the eyes of the other young man which reminded her of two pools of clear blue water and she felt herself being pulled down into their depths.

He was of medium height with broad shoulders. His arm muscles bunched up like egg sized stones beneath the skin as he lifted the log. Isabel first decided his eyes were blue but when she viewed them from another angle they were a smoky gray with tiny golden flecks but again, standing near him she saw they were clear as the sky above their heads and green as deep sea water.

His hair was sandy and needed cutting but his most attractive features, with the exception of his eyes, were his thick luxuriant beard and mustache which instead of being sandy like his hair were a glossy reddish brown. His quick friendly smile revealed white even teeth and his fair skin was touched with a golden shade from being outside so much and she noticed as he wiped sweat from his face that his fingers were long and slender.

Isabel smelled flowers that had not as yet even budded. The fragrance of lilac and roses were most prevalent, being her favorite flowers. Lizzie Beth gouged her in the ribs with her elbow bringing her back to the world of reality, "That's my baby brother you're alooking at," she whispered and rolled her eyes in a comical way until they looked like blue half-moons. "Be sure you look only at him, the other one is mine!" Isabel and Lizzie Beth moved on a few paces pretending to be interested in the work the other men were doing but soon they found themselves retracing their steps as if being drawn by a magnet to where the two young men were heaving and puffing trying to lift another log. One of the men called down to the girls to bring them some water. As they passed the drinking gourd around Isabel noticed a tall dark slender young man eyeing them as she handed him the dipper and she saw he was handsome in a sinister kind of way. There was no nod or smile of greeting from his thin cruel lips and for some unknown reason she felt a shiver run up and down her spine.

As they moved on Lizzie Beth whispered behind her hand, "That's Rolland Borak, he lives high up on the side of the mountain all by his lonesome." Lizzie Beth raised her hands in a waving motion toward one of the northern slopes. "Granny and Grand Pap raised him. I'll have Granny tell you about him ater we eat."

After hanging around the two young men as long as possible without embarrassing themselves, the girls returned to the house where Isabel took a quick mental inventory of its interior. It was plain to see someone in the family had been or was handy with wood carving. Two wooden bedsteads made from curly maple stood in the far corners of the big living room, beautifully carved in intricate designs. Large wooden spoons hung below the carved mantel and a long wooden chain with a swivel end hung from a peg in the wall. The house had a split log floor and an over head ceiling hewn as smooth as hard work and patience could make them. The rough places the hewer had left in the floor time had finished with the aid of the scrub-broom.

Two black bear skins met in the center between the beds and a ladder led up into the loft where Isabel supposed Lizzie Beth slept. The house had two doors, two porches and two shuttered windows in the end where the cooking was done on the fireplace.

Isabel turned her attention to the elderly woman. Granny Cook's hair was rolled in a large bun on the top of her head, where black strands still streaked the silver tresses. Her hands though wrinkled with age looked soft and tender, since she had ceased working in the fields the calluses and roughness had healed.

She was plump as a pigeon and her full bosom reached below her skirt band and judging from her facial bone structure Isabel could see she had once been a beautiful woman.

Lizzie Beth's mother needed something from the old trunk that sat against the foot board of one of the beds. While Lizzie Beth rummaged through its contents Isabel's mind, active as a bee-hive flitted in all directions. She wondered whose hands had done the carving, she wondered about the strange man with the cold eyes who lived alone on the mountain, she wondered about Lizzie Beth and her young man but most of all she wondered about Lizzie Beth's good looking brother.

The thud of the closing trunk lid snapped her out of her wool-gathering. One of the women told the girls it was time to carry the food out to were a flat bedded wagon swept clean waited to serve as a table. The girls with much fluster and twittering fell into the task whole heartedly knowing they had to pass the two young men each trip.

After the delicious food had been devoured and the giggling and flirting was over and the men were back at their work, the women scattered about the yard discussing flower beds and garden spots. After the dishes were washed and put away by the girls, they pulled split-bottomed chairs near to where old Granny sat full and contented beside the hearth.

The Boraks

Old Granny smiled at the two girls and wiped her mouth on her apron tail, then began her story about the Boraks. "We wuz atraveling with sum other wagons when we come to where the trail forked at the foot uv the mountains, nart one uv us had never been in these here parts afore and alooking up at the high and rugged mountain made a body feel kinda fearful, so being dog tired we decided to make camp early and git a little rest afore tackling the road ahead."

"Well, a wagon that had been astraggling behind all day drove up and pulled over on the tother side uv the road where we wuz acamping and the driver, a big stoop shouldered man in his middle years crossed the road and started atalking to the men folks. I looked over toward the other wagon and there stood the purtiest woman I ever did see. She had big dark eyes, black hair and skin as white as milk."

"Her man was tall, slim and dark and the woman wuz aholding a small child in her arms and that wuz not all I seed. I looked to where a smoke wuz arising beyond the wagon and a nigger woman as black as midnight wuz abuilding a far."

"Then I turned my attention to what the driver uv the wagon wuz atelling the men folks. He said they were of French descent and they had come from that furrin country from across the water and had lived on a big plantation that wuz worked by slaves."

He said, "The couple had wanted to git married but her Pap had put his foot down and ferbid them to do so, so they ist run away an got married enyway. They took with them the old nigger woman that had waited on her since she wuz little an they had headed fer the high country but when she found out she wuz agoing to have a baby they changed their plans fer a spell, hiding out in the low lands afeared all the time her Pap would catch up with em. Well, that nigger woman shore put a damper on things. It wuz plain none uv the other travelers wanted to bring a nigger into the new land they wanted to settle in. Well, after supper things livened up. Some of the men got to amaking music on the fiddle an banger and afore you could say scat most everybody wuz adancing an cutin up. The old nigger woman took the little youngun into the wagon and that wuz the last we seed uv her, then the young couple started adancing on the other side uv the road. I declare I can est see her now, dancing in her little fancy shoes the likes I have never seed afore and her long full skirt billering out around her as her man swung her around in the air as ifen she wuz as light as a feather."

"When the young couple got all tuckered out from all that dancing they bowed to us all, then they went awalking beneath the timber hand in hand. Later on when the shadders had deepened we heard screams acoming from their wagon and the woman comes atearing out as ifen the devil wuz ater her, her man tried to hold her but she wuz acting like a crazy person."

"About that time the child in the wagon began to wail. I waited for the nigger woman to do sompen but when its wails got louder and louder I climbed in the wagon to see why the old woman didn't stop the child from acrying."

"Well, I shore got a shaking up, that old nigger woman wuz as dead as Sam Hider's dog and stiffer than a poker. No wonder that little child wuz ascreaming hits head off! Hit wuz the strangest sicheation I had ever come across, and to cap it all off the men had to dig a grave. We wrapped her up in a blanket and buried her neath a big oak tree by the light uv our campfire."

Old Granny smiled at the two girls. She wiped her mouth on her apron tail and continued her story about the Boraks.

"The next morning wuz a sad time fer all uv us. We had made up our minds to take the left fork and all the others we had been traveling with decided on the right prong. Due to my aknowing how to raise younguns and me ataking the little chile under my wing, so to speak, during the night, the young couple wanted to travel with us so as I could help take care uv hit along the trail."

"It wuz ruf traveling trying to git to the top of the mountain. The trail had been traveled by Indians and animals but nary a wheel had teched hit an hit had to be widened all the way, an we sure wuz a weary bunch."

"We camped fer a spell ater crossing the river an rested up, chopping an fendering the road wuz taking hits toll on the men folkses but things got better ater that. The minute I stepped through the gap and looked down over the field I knowed I had found the place I wanted to settle down."

"That little furrin girl cried ever step uv the way. She didn't know a thing about ataking care uv that baby fer the old black woman had taken care uv hit since hits birth but I took over hit's care on the trail and when she stepped through the gap and viewed the mountains and the vales she perked right up." She gazed up at the Fork Mountain and said, "Here's a place where one could be swallowed up forever."

Seldom did old Granny attract such an attentive audience. She decided to detour from the Borak's story and fill in a few missing links in her own family history. "Well, we camped here an the men started achopping down trees fer a building, I sez to them, we need a barn. Build hit first an we can live in hit till you-uns can build me a proper house, an that is what they done."

"We tried to get the Boraks to settle near us, seeing they had nobody to help them, but she said she hoped the mountains would swaller them up ferever, as it turned out that is what they done. They went up on the mountain above Dogwood Flats and settled there."

"After our barn wuz built and the Borak's cabin raised the men said we had to have a building for the live-stock, so they ups and builds us a small log house. That's hit out back with the grapevines growing over hit. We use hit now to store my split baskets, yarbs and hickory bark, an there's part of that old curley maple tree my man stored years ago. He wuz a natural builder an carver."

Granny paused for a moment and stared out through the open window, the shutter had a small hole in its upper corner and a piece of raw-hide was stuck through the hole and looped over a wooden peg holding it secure to the wall. The girls knew old Granny was viewing another world at that moment, so they waited patiently for her to snap back to the present.

Suddenly, her bright, though faded eyes focused on the girls again and she smiled. "Well, to git back to the Boraks. One day I went up there and she showed me her things she had brought all the way from the lowlands. She had a dress with a high collar and pearl buttons all the way down to her waist. What ever kind uv truck hit was made out uv I'll never know but hit wuz shiny like and had a big full skirt."

"I asked her to put hit on and she did. She had a pair uv little shoes with heels an I declare I never did see the like. She looked like a queen in em clothes."

Granny stopped for a second to get her wind back and swallowed, then continued. "I didn't tell you about her long hair. Well, when she combed hit out hit reached almost to the floor. Never in all my born days did I ever see so much hair on a human head, an hit shined like a raven's wing when tetched by the sun."

"Rolland wuz a lively little youngun then. He played all by hisself on the hill above the house an I remember well as ifen hit wuz yestey the big log he kept crawling through. I told him a big black snake would get him fer sure ifen he didn't stay out uv that log."

"The spring when Rolland wuz three years old we wuz aplanting corn up in the field above here. We had planted almost to the top an we looked up on the slope of the mountain where the Boraks lived and a big smoke wuz curling up through the timber, an we could see the blaze ashooten up in the air as the buildings burned."

"The men drapped their hoes an run as hard as they could to get to the horses. I thought hit might be Indians, so I run all the way down here an gathered the rest of the family together, an we took off across the field to where the Indian trail leads down from the gap in the mountain. We crossed the trail and hid in a laurel thicket. We carried all we could from the house for we feared ifen hit wuz Indians our buildings would go up in flames too."

"Well, I climbed up to where I could see the mountains and squatted behind a big rock where I waited. Finally I seed the men come out uv the timber and hit the road. The others crawled out uv their hiding places and we took off through the field agin and met the men there."

"My man wuz aholding little Rolland in his arms. Hit is hard fer a grown man to cry but my men-folks wuz acrying like women, an I knowed there wuz bad trouble, an I sez, "What about Rolland's folks?" "My man ist kept on acrying an apatting, and smoothing little Rolland's clothes. Then he put the child down on a rock, an he never moved or cried or anything."

"We walked out uv the boy's hearen an my man said, "they air both dead, they wuz kilt by stinking Indians." Then I sez, though it wuz hard to ask, did they get her hair?" My man looked down at his feet fer a long time an I thought maybe he didn't hear me. Then he told me, they scalped them, then hacked them to pieces, then they set the house an barn on fire. The boy wuz aplayin in the woods above the house. When he seed the Indians, he crawled into the big hollow log above the house an watched them kill his people. When he seed us he crawled out."

Old Granny threw up her hands, "Let me tell you, I wuz never as scart in my life! The men took their guns and tools up there and buried what wuz left uv the poor things, an we kept little Rolland an raised him until he wuz about fourteen. Then he went back up the mountain an built another cabin with the help uv my men-folks, where the other one had been."

At this point the old woman lowered her voice and glanced toward the door, "Rolland wuz never right after the killing. We never seed him eny more cept when we need hep, like with this here barn raising. He est seems to know when to come. I know I should regard him as my own after raising him an all, but," Granny's voice trailed off and she looked at her hands that were folded in her lap and her face wore a pensive expression.

Isabel felt a deep pang of sympathy for her. The young Borak's tragic and untimely deaths had affected the old lady's life so much she could see the scars would never heal.

Presently Granny rallied again and continued her story. "There wuz only one other man in this valley at that time, your brother John, he wuz aliving in a little pole cabin further up the road than where he now lives. That wuz some time afore he got married."

"Rolland wuz awful young to be by hisself, though a lot uv boys git married at that age but to go back on that mountain an live on the very same spot where his folks wuz kilt an knowing the danger he wuz afacing seemed peculiar to me. His parents had gone up in that place where they wuz no protection at all, an they wouldn't listen to us older folks who could see the danger they wuz awalking into."

"But Rolland knowed first hand the danger he faced, an still he went. Well, several years passed an nothing happened to him. He kept to his self, an we respected his privysee."

"Then one day after a few years had passed two settlers wuz ahuntin on the mountain above the Borak place. They had skirted the cabin, fer as time passed strange tales began to circulate about Rolland's place, so no one dared to venture near his cabin."[7]

"Now, the two hunters wuz hunkered down in the bushes near the animal trail that leads down offen the mountain. All of a sudden a deer bounded off the trail, an liked to arun over them, an afore they could raise their guns the deer had disappeared."

"Well, the men knowed somepen had startled the deer, so they remained as quite as mice an waited. They didn't have to wait long, somepen wuz amoving on the game trail a few yards west of where they wuz hunkered down."

"Then a band of Indians passed on the trail, walking single file," old Granny paused in her story telling long enough to go to the fireplace and spit. She reached up on the mantle and picked up a length of dried grapevine which she lit in the embers. Isabel had seen old Granny Ann do the same thing many times before she came to John's valley. It was supposed to be a remedy for sinus.

After returning to her chair she took several puffs of the grapevine smoke, while Isabel waited on pins and needles to hear the rest of the story.

"Now this is the way hit wuz told to me by the very men this happened to. "They said one of them nodded at the other, then crept to the edge of the trail, then motioning at the other feller they slipped from the bushes an onto the trail."

"Now these wuz seasoned mountain men, stealthy as any Indian ever wuz. They follered to see what the Indians wuz up to, being careful not to be seen."

"Indians haint been seen since the killing that low on the mountain slopes. They follered the main trails along the high mountain tops an they shunned the trails that lead into this valley."

"The men told me they felt uneasy in the pits uv their stomachs, with ist the two of them agin a bunch of Indians, so they wuz doubly careful. The Indians seemed to know exactly where they were agoin, an the two men got more uneasy when they left the trail an headed east through the woods toward the Borak place."

"The settlers retraced their steps up the trail to a safe distance, then follered higher up through the woods, picking their way very careful like until they reached a wet weather

---

[7] The old Goff place up on the side of the mountain is the place where the Indians murdered the Borak couple. There are still signs of the foundation and chimney stack. A hewn log cabin was later erected after Rolland Borak passed on to his final reward. Lonny Cook was the last one to live there with his family. Steven Cook needed logs for a barn and Thomas Ledford, Steven's brother-in-law, needed a right-of-way over Steven's land so they shook hands on the deal and Steven tore down the cabin at the Goff place and built a barn. There is still a faint sign of the old wagon road that Thomas used while he lived on the mountain above Dogwood Flats.

branch. Lucky fer them the water still trickled due to a recent rain fall. You know, it's a funny thing, you can step on a dry limb out in the woods an it cracks almost as loud as a pistol shot. An you can hear it ever so fer an heaven help you ifen there's Indians within yere shot."

"So the settlers walked in the shallow trickle of water where the limbs wuz soaked an would not snap like the ones on the floor of the woods. As you know, Indians has herein as keen as a varmint. When they hear a sound they est seem to fade away right afore your eyes, an the next thing you know they're at your back ready to crack your skull with them tomahawks they carry."

"They ist seem to tune in to ever little sound when they're out in the mountains. Guess us folks don't pay enough attention to things. Well, the settlers said they snuck down the water course an hid in the bushes where they had a clear view of Rolland's place. Below his cabin the earth ist falls away forming a steep embankment."

"According to the two men the Indians peeped over the embankment, an hit wuz plain they meant to do harm to the place but when they seen the long black Indian hair swinging back an forth in the wind which wuz tied to long poles that wuz stuck in the ground, the sight throwed them Indians into a panic. They turned an high tailed it out of there as if the furies wuz after them."

Old Granny lowered her head and looked up through her eye brows straight at the girls. Her gaze was so sharp and penetrating it seemed to Isabel that Granny was seeing right through her skull and analyzing every thought that ran through her brain.

"Well, they said ater the Indians disappeared through the timber they crept out uv their hiding place an walked down to the Borak cabin. They said the place had sech a creepy feeling about it both of them felt chills crawl up an down their spines."

"Boards, like the ones used to stretch varmint hides on wuz also swinging from poles stuck in the ground." Once again, Granny paused, then lowering her voice almost to a whisper she continued, "only it twarent varmint hides, the skins on them boards wuz different, there wuz no hair on em."

"Varmint hides is always stretched with the fur turned inside so the pelts will cure out but the fur can be seen around the edges, but not in this case. The skins only kivered one side uv the boards, an wuz lashed together on the back side with raw-hide throngs, and the skins wuz as smooth as the back of yer hand."

Old Granny tapped the back of her hand with a knobby forefinger to get the message across to the girls who were by that time shaking like a leaf in an autumn breeze. "After seeing the scalps an skins the settlers come to their own conclusions. They said they left that place almost as fast as the Indians had."

Old Granny stirred in her chair, this had been a long story telling session. One she had thoroughly enjoyed. She had watched while emotions played over Isabel's countenance as plain as the light and shadows on the high mountains when the wind rustles their colors in autumn.

Before rising she pointed her finger at the girls and shook it before their faces, "I'll tell you this! Don't ever climb that mountain, there's things to be heard up there like moaning and screaming. Maybe the place is hanted or maybe hit's screaming Indians being skinned alive. Them skins has to come from some where!"

"I used to think them screams come from Rolland's own throat, living all alone an seeing his people kilt over an over in his mind but them strange skins sheds a different light on things." Suddenly Isabel felt faint, the wicked hunting knife Rolland had used on the meat at their noon time meal flashed sickeningly through her mind and she closed her eyes against the nausea that threatened to engulf her.

Kindred Spirits

Lizzie Beth jumped to her feet and grabbed Isabel's arm. "Come on, I'll show you the loft where I sleep. You look as white as a ghost any way!" Grateful for the interruption Isabel followed numbly, her senses dulled by the shocking events old Granny had revealed to her.

The loft was dark and warm and Isabel needed warmth. A coldness had crept over her and seeped down, it seemed, to her very bone marrow. Lizzie Beth told her to wait until she opened the shutters and as the light streamed in she could see four bed-ticks, one in each corner.

Sheep skins were spread on the floor beside the beds and Lizzie Beth threw herself down on one of the beds in the west end of the loft and motioned for Isabel to do the same. The girls lay silent for a while, enjoying the close comradeliness and looked up at the dark over head covering that peaked in the center like a giant hog-trough turned upside down.

"You know", Lizzie Beth said after a while, "I like to git up at night and look out the winder at the stars and sky. One night the moon wuz big and bright, outside ever thing wuz shiny looking, like a different place from what hit is in day light, an as I looked two big black shadders started aplaying in the field."

"I watched fer a long time as they jumped an frolicked around. I thought they act ist like kittens aplaying then hit struck me, them two shadders must be panters an I got the shutter fastened fast."

"I crawled through the floor an fastened the shutter in the other end uv this here loft where my brother sleeps, then I yelled down to Paw an told him what I'd seen. Ems panthers fer certen", he said. By then ever body in the house wuz awake and Maw blowed up the fire she had banked an they lit some pine knot torches. We keep a pile uv em on both porches. Well, all uv us carried em burning torches outside an Paw lit a big log-heap he had piled in the field. Varmints is afraid uv far you know. Then he tied the dogs out in the barn an they started abarking an ahowling with their tails between their legs like they wuz scared to death."

"We hurd the panters ascreaming higher and higher in the mountains till the sound ist faded out. Paw said, they wuz aheadin fer the big cliff high up in the mountains where they den."

The two girls switched from one subject to another, the versatility of their conversation covered a lot of ground as it glided back and forth between Isabel's childhood in the Blue Ridge and Lizzie Beth's past and present.

Lizzie Beth kicked off her moccasins and spread her toes wide, then propped her head with her hand with elbow resting on the bed-tick and looked at Isabel. "You know my sister's got a hole passel uv younguns an her girl Rose Ann is a year older than me. The reason none uv em come to the barn raising today wuz because my sister's in the family-way again an feeling poorly an that Rose Ann! She sticks her nose in the air ever time she sees me lately. She sez I took her feller. Well, he lives over near where she lives, the only neighbors they have closer 'n us, an ifen she can't hold him then that's her loss, not mine!"

"Maw has ferbid me to go with him because uv Rose Ann" but Lizzie Beth giggled and rolled her eyes. "My sister is acoming here to stay in a week or two until after the birthing. So, with all the goings on, an me run out uv the house an all, fer they won't let me near the house when Granny sez it's time, an she fastens the doors. You know? She is more than my Granny, she's a granny woman."[8]

Isabel reflected briefly on the news that old Granny Cook was a mid-wife until Lizzie Beth's voice cut into her thoughts. "Rose Ann will be acooking fer the family over there while my sister is here. She had better put that feller uv her's in her pocket an draw the puckering string real tight fer I intend to have my man before this time next year, even ifen hit means aliving in Granny's old house where she hangs her yarbs."

Isabel looked at Lizzie Beth and both girls hid their heads beneath the covers to muffle the sound of their giggles. At last, after being alone amid a large family clan, Isabel had found a kindred spirit.

---

[8] Old time name for a midwife.

Spring's Awakening

Spring had come full blown to the mountains with the promise of summer unfolding on the hills and in the valleys. The blue and purple ranges formed a perfect background for the pastel colors that ran depths of medium to light yellowish green on the larger timber.

Soon it would be a sea of deep green when the foliage thickened. Beneath the tall trees lesser shrubbery bloomed in wild perfusion in shades ranging from the pale shell pink of the sarvess blooms to the deeper color of the wild hawthorn.

The near crimson color of the crab-apple flowers sent waves of fragrance wafting on gentle breezes.

The coming spring had broken the last thin threads of childhood that had clung like gossamer strands to Isabel's young life. Now she was treading on uncharted shores of adulthood, thrown there by circumstance and perhaps destiny.

As a sailor casts up on a foreign strand without a compass while in search of the lay of the land and walks boldly unaware of quick-sand pits hidden beneath the deceiving beauty of the strange terrain. So she waked on that day in her fifteenth year, mindful only of the alluring song of the ages. Lyrics that all young people hear only once, clear sounding as a crystal bell. Notes that call like the pipes of pan and the heart must follow, for the sounding is brief and only echoes have to suffice after the music dies away.

Isabel was ill equipped to face life's jungle frontier with its winding paths and hidden dangers. All the women folk in the family clan talked in riddles and if she were caught listening too closely, their eyelids would drop and their eyes would take on a veiled look. She would usually be sent on an unnecessary errand, like to the spring for fresh water which no one tasted when she returned. So she knew they had used the water for an excuse to get her out of hearing.

Isabel would never forget the time when she was twelve. She had tried to find out in her awkward way a few facts of life from old Granny Ann, who was the mid-wife of their section and mother-in-law to her dead sister, but the old woman had been so brusque in letting her know things of that nature was none of her affair. As the old woman's eyes, small and black as Indian beads, scanned her from head to toe she had stood mortified. She felt as if she had invaded the sacred halls of some strange and secret cult.

The spring planting was over and in the pause between planting and hoeing John's new house of hewn popular logs was being raised. Isabel's kin from the Blue Ridge had arrived and the place was alive with activity. Since the day of the barn raising Isabel had floated around in a daze. So may exciting things had happened, her cup over flowed with the joy of it all. First there was her new friend and confidant, Lizzie Beth, who romped with her through the woods and hills in their spare time despite warnings from both families.

The only thing that sent fear coursing through her being was Rolland Borak. It seemed she could feel eyes following her every where she went alone but the fear was soon forgotten when she was in the company of Lizzie Beth.

It was as if her life, like flood gates, had been closed and now were open. She was free to flow unhampered through courses new and wonderful. Lizzie Beth had told her that her brother had been "sweet" on another girl before she came to the valley. "She's my feller's sister and good looking but not down right purty like you. His props wuz knocked right out from under him from the minute he laid eyes on you. He follers me around like a sick calf askin all kinds of questions about you." Isabel felt her face burn and said, "you're joshing

Lizzie Beth." "Joshing my foot1 You two locked eyes like two young bulls locking horns," Lizzie Beth giggled and skipped along. "I can fix hit so's you two can see each other. You know that place where you like to set an look at the water in the bend of the creek? Be there a little afore dark after the evening work is done. Hit won't give you much time to get acquainted but that's the best time uv day to slip away from the house. Believe me, I know!"

From that day on Lizzie Beth served as go-between. Messages passed back and forth and soon the creek bank became the trysting place for the two young lovers. Sunday afternoons were spent roaming the hills with hands entwined often accompanied by Lizzie Beth and her feller as she always referred to him.

The two couples talked back and forth about their future plans. Being secret lovers seemed more exciting some how with just the four of them sharing each others hopes and dreams.

One Sunday's excursion ended up in Dogwood Flats. Isabel fell in love with the place at first sight. The dogwoods bloomed white like piles of snow and the wind moaned softly through their branches as if in pain because of the over crowding joy it could not contain.

Isabel picked out the spot where her future home would be near a bubbling spring. A place where no living human being had ever lived before. This valley nestled beneath the sheltering shadow of the Fork Mountain bluff belonged to her and the man she loved as surely as the sun rose each morning.

By the time the logs were finally raised and the top was covered on John's new house, it was time for the first corn hoeing. Isabel's and Lizzie Beth's folks had decided to swap work that summer, much to the delight of the young people. Isabel worked along beside her young man unmindful of the sweat that streaked her dusty face and plastered her hair to her scalp beneath her bonnet. Before going to the house after quitting time, Isabel always took the path to the creek and bathed in the cold creek water. Her teeth chattered as she sank into the chilling depths but the refreshing feeling of being clean was more than rewarding. She would soak up the late evening sun. In its warmth she would spread her hair to dry. Isabel's young man never ceased to be amazed at her freshness when they met and roamed in the twilight.

Her lustrous hair waved and curled in ringlets from its recent immersion in the creek. It looked as black as a raven's wing beneath the timber. It had shone like a red halo as she crossed the field to where he was waiting, touched by the last bright sun rays of the day.

Spring had blended into early summer and then slipped gracefully as a ballet dancer into the season's deepest heat. Isabel reveled in it all because life for her was in full bloom. She swam in the big creek where the water holes were deep and treacherous, where tree laps washed in by heavy rains lurked beneath the surface and waited to snare her reckless feet.

She felt there was more danger in the changeable eyes of the young man who had become her whole reason for living than there would have been if she had wadded in old Toe River at flood stage.

The new house, almost finished now, had lost its meaning for her. Lizzie Beth's friendship was pushed gently into the background where Lizzie Beth was perfectly content to be. She was as busy as an old hen herself, hatching schemes for her future nest. Nothing mattered to Isabel but the fact she would soon be living for the rest of her natural life in a hidden valley shadowed by a great forked bluff with the man of her choice. But no one can foresee when Apropos will use her scissors, for the threads of life are fragile, least of all Isabel on that fatal day when her dreams ended as suddenly as they had begun.

For Whom The Doves Mourn

Swinging axes broke the silence of a perfect summer morn as a group of men matched their strength against each other. Piles of chips accumulated at their feet as the big tree took on the appearance of having been gnawed by a giant beaver.

Timber grew thick and plentiful everywhere in this new wilderness area and the need for logs, though not as great as the bountiful supply, was almost limitless.

Attracted by the vigor of the chopping in which two men were engaged, the rest of the group gathered around to watch the contest of strength. Bets were made as to who would become winded first and the men cheered as the axes struck in steady rhythm.

With sweat streaked faces the two chopped until due to the proper notching, the great tree fell true but a dead giant of a chestnut tree stood near by with a huge twisted limb that rose upward. As if in supplication to the heavens against nature's ravages, it was torn loose from the trunk by the sweeping branches of the felled tree and came crashing down with thunderous force to strike its last fierce blow before lying earth bound forever.

Beneath its weight a young man lay, as if asleep, the eyes were closed and the face relaxed. No broken bones protruded and no blood spurted to wet the earth where he lay. He had died instantly from a broken neck.

Old Granny Cook had saved what was left of the curly maple wood after the bed steeds had been made and the mantle carved. It had been her plan to have a coffin made for herself because the huge tree had been cut by her dead husband's own hands but now that the shock of the tragedy had rendered the rest of the family incapable of thinking or planning a funeral, she took charge.

Her grief was deep and painful for she not only mourned for her beloved grandson but for Isabel and her crushed dreams as well. But Granny had always been able to face up to what ever forces life had to bring, so she asked John to ride to the Blue Ridge where the main portion of his family still lived and bring back his kin folk to help dig the grave and to make the coffin.

The burial had to be hasty for the heat hovered over the mountains in unusual fierceness, so much so, the corn blades twisted on the stalks and the cattle took to the deep woods in order to seek relief.

Like all wilderness communities, a graveyard was an ever present necessity. The hand of death had already appeared several times to snatch away both young and old alike.

Strange as it may seem, it had never occurred to Granny Cook to start a family burial place some where in the big field below the gap. Instead she had chosen a gently rolling knoll a short distance up the trail that led into Dogwood Flats. Her infant son had been the first to be buried there beneath the towering trees. Several more infants throughout the family followed and last of all her husband.

Granny considered the situation from all angles. The family and friends had to be fed and the cooking had to be done on the fireplace. So with John's permission she had the corpse dressed and carried to his new and as yet unoccupied house where it lay until the funeral.

Again Rolland Borak appeared like a spectrum out of the mists and set to work on the coffin. As a boy he had watched Granny's husband split and carve wood but never to any one's knowledge had he ever set his hands to the task. Now he directed the men in the splitting then he worked and pegged the beautiful old wood into a coffin more splendid than anyone in the present section had ever seen.

Isabel on hearing the shocking news had felt as if she were really drowning. She sank down, it seemed, into a quagmire of quick sand and felt herself sucked down into its murky depths.

Like Niobe, she felt cold as if turned to stone but her tears still flowed. It was Granny who reached her numbed spirit and offered a measure of comfort. Lizzie Beth took to the loft and her bed. Isabel had refused until the last hour before the funeral to look at the coffin or corpse but old Granny in her wisdom after clearing the house took her by the arm and led her inside and closed the door against curious eyes and turned the button.

Guiding her to the coffin she raised the cloth from her Grandson's face and dropped it into a bowl of camphor water. As the strong sickening scent of the camphor rose to her nostrils Isabel opened her eyes. Her young man lay looking much as he looked in life except the deep tan that had made his teeth seem so white was gone and the pallor of death had taken its place.

The camphor had kept his face from settling except for a dark streak that started below his left cheek bone and ran down his neck to his shirt collar.

Isabel stood transfixed. Her brain could not accept the fact that this was the last time she would ever see his face again. Her shattered thoughts flitted about like a moth around a flame as old Granny let go of her arm and walked across the room to give her a few minutes alone with her dead.

Granny plucked a single bloom from a bunch of flowers she had gathered earlier to place on the coffin when it closed for the last time. She gently brushed her fingers across the soft petals then laid it aside to be pressed in the family bible.

Isabel involuntarily reached down to take a lock of the sandy hair but stopped the gesture in mid-air. Everything seemed so futile at that moment.

Little did she know at that time she carried a living momentum that would ever be a reminder of the young man who now lay so quite and still in death and who would never awake as the bible said,

> Till the heavens be no more, they shall not awake,
> nor be raised out of their sleep.

Fate had dealt her a terrible blow. It had taken a life and in return a new one would take its place before the late spring snows melted from the high peaks and the dogwoods bloomed again on the hills.

Strength from an unknown source from deep within rose to the surface of her mind and she knew she had touched a depth so deep that no matter what happened in the future nothing could compare with the stroke life had dealt her at this time.

After the last shovel of dirt had been heaped on the grave and the last mourner and friend had paid their last respects and quietly with bowed heads left the hill where only their foot prints in the red clay witnessed they had ever been there, Isabel stood alone on the little knoll. The bunches of flowers already looked wilted in the sweltering heat and she listened to the wind that had sung and sighed in the spring but now moaned and cried in the tree tops, heralding the approaching storm and the mourning doves' lonely call echoed among the hills and she knew for whom they were mourning.

Young George

On a lovely Sunday morning in mid September a young man stood in the edge of the big field where his mother Isabel had stood so long ago when she first came to the valley and saw a vision that went back into the misty past to an Indian village that once existed there and viewed his surroundings with pleasure.

The popular leaves were golden yellow as if each one of them had felt the touch of Midas's golden fingers. Sugar trees and maples burned bright forecasting the colors of flames that would soon flash fiery red on the hearth-stones of this new land.

Already the frost had scattered its chilly breath over the fields. Many leaves, unable to withstand the hot sun rays after the biting cold, had slipped from the trees and lay scattered in bright colored splashes on the ground.

Possum grapes hung in tangled clusters in the timber along the edge of the field awaiting a few more frosty nights to bring out their rich, wild flavor. Already the grape arbors the settlers had planted had passed their prime and now the grapes hung juicy, wet and half flayed of their thick hulls by the pesky yellow jackets.

Grasses and weeds that had only a few days previous thrived in their many shades of green now lay prostrate on the earth in colors of raw umber.

The young man turned his head and looked at the little log church that crouched low and inviting like a mother hen waiting to hover her chicks. Indeed each time he entered and stood beneath its hallowed roof it seemed to him as if he were sheltered by comforting wings.

His eyes bore the look of a dreamer, the color hard to define, but now in the shimmering morning sun they were a smoky blue-gray color like the morning mists against the blue mountains.

His thick lustrous hair was the color of a buckeye that had fallen and cured on the ground from a bright glossy shade to a dark rich brown that appeared almost black except when touched by the sun.

He was of medium height and build and his skin though tanned was fair and smooth as a woman's. His hands strong and callused by hard work bespoke of gentleness and his whole manner set him apart from the other mountain men.[9]

As he stood there alone near the little church a brisk breeze swept across the bottom. As it rose from the dry grasses of the field to the tree tops its voice low and rasping among the dying leaves sounded like the death rattle of summer as it fought its way through the thick timber. Then whispered and moaned in softer tones on the slopes beyond.

Suddenly the world was quiet, not a breeze moved. Then the pitter-patter of softly falling leaves could be heard. Each sight and sound of this day was to be a treasured memory, painted in fadeless colors on the canvas of his mind, for this was his wedding day.

After the wedding ceremony he was taking his bride Betsy to the new house that was ready and waiting for them in the little hidden valley of Dogwood Flats.

For a moment his mind turned back to this childhood and for a fleeting moment he felt a touch of guilt, as if his own hopes and plans had sprung from the ashes of his mother's crushed dreams.

---

[9] George's age shown on the census makes his birth around 1818 and his death was in 1888.

He shook his head as if to clear away the strange thoughts that crowded his mind. After all it had been Isabel who had taken him each summer on long excursions to the flats. Oft times they stood together on the old sand hill west of Dogwood Flats in early spring and viewed the loveliness before them.

Of all the flowering trees and shrubs such as sarvis, wild azaleas and wild hawthorns, the dogwoods were more abundant. They bloomed like mounds of snow over the landscape concealing beneath their flowering beauty much of the rough terrain.

As he had grown older his frequent excursions all by his lonesome had strengthened his determination to someday live in Dogwood Flats. Once when barely a teenager he had left the flats and climbed the mountain to the north of the valley and spied on Rolland Borak from his hiding place in the rough to the right of the clearing where the Borak cabin nestled like a bird's nest against the ridge.

He had crawled on hands and knees among the boulders and when the Borak cabin came into view he had slithered around on his stomach like a garter snake until finally he found a good position near the edge of a branch which flowed briskly over the rocks for several yards, then rushed madly down the mountain as if in a great hurry to reach the larger streams beyond the valley.

There on the north side of a big rock he lay as still as the huge boulder beside him, hardly daring to breathe. Honey bees watered at the edge of the branch opposite his hiding place and he had wished he had brought along some corn meal in his pocket. The settlers used this method to judge the distance between the water and the bee tree after sprinkling meal on the bees backs and watching the course of their flight. It was easy to judge the distance the bees had flown when they returned to their watering places with the dry meal still on their backs.

George had become so engrossed with the bees he had not seen Rolland come out of the cabin. When he next looked in that direction Rolland was standing in the yard, something cold as ice water flooded through his being as the man turned to face in his direction. He watched as Rolland squatted in the yard. He was not close enough to see what he was occupied with but he could see some kind of object suspended in the air. Now and then it moved in a ghostly fashion when the wind stirred in the trees.

Perhaps it was just an old animal pelt but he had heard so many grizzly tales about the place it made his blood run cold as a mountain spring, the hairs on his head stood up and he felt the goose flesh crawl over his body.

It had seemed an eternity before the man rose to his feet and returned to his cabin. George had seized the opportunity to slither backwards until he was out of sight of the cabin and its sinister occupant. Then he had fled from the place never to return in Rolland's lifetime.

His mind slipped from one experience of his boyhood to another as fluid as the waters that flowed in the cold creek bed behind him. Early in life he had found his calling. Different preachers had rode into the valley during his growing up years and a large stump near the creek in the western edge of the field had served as a pulpit.

Stump meetings were warm weather occurrences and settlers from miles around attended. Then one day in later spring a preacher rode through the gap in the mountain. He was different from the other preachers who had preceded him. He had a way with words and the beautiful psalms read in the new preacher's flowing manner had held him spell bound.

It was during that revival meeting that he had made up his mind to learn to read. So with long hours of study and the help of the preacher during his stay in the valley, he had mastered his most cherished dream to the extent that with study and perseverance he was able to conquer a whole new world.

The new preacher had made the settlers feel ashamed as he told them to lift up their eyes unto the hills, then asked a question, "Are there not trees on every ridge and hill and in every valley, have you not built houses and barns but where is your house of worship? Is there not a need for services in the winter as well as summer but who can preach from a stump when the snow is deep and white in this valley? Many of you can not read. Will you bring your families to stand in the harsh winter weather to listen to the words from the bible?" Then the preacher paused and looked out over the crowd of people and said in a solemn voice, "Where there is no vision, the people perish."

Before the next winter storm swept over the waters of Little Rock Creek a new log church stood proudly in the edge of the big field not far from the place where his mother Isabel had stood as a young girl when she first arrived in the valley.

The church was complete with a fireplace and enough wood to last through the cold season and a hitching pole so the settlers could hitch up their horses during services.

From that summer on time had passed swiftly and happily for young George. He had been ordained in the Baptist faith and the little church bore the title Fork Mountain Baptist Church over its door.

If he could have glimpsed into the far future at that time his mind could not have grasped the vision his eyes beheld, or the great changes that were to take place during the long years that lay ahead for future generations. The little log church with its humble beginning was destined to lay in ashes several years hence and a new church, weather boarded and painted white was to set along side the wagon road that led down Little Rock Creek instead of in the edge of the big field near the cold waters of the little creek that would someday bear his name.

If the misty clouds of time could have vanished and the future could have been revealed on a screen on the far horizon up until the present time his mind would have rebelled in unbelief at the sight of a modern brick church complete with a baptistery and fellowship hall with a paved parking lot and highway.

As it was he could not see beyond the present which lay before him warm and inviting like a table spread and waiting and he had only to reach out and be filled with its bountiful goodness.

Then a vision of an earlier time passed before his eyes so real even the warm sun on his face could not dispel the chill that swept over his being. It was as if a dark cloud had blotted out the warmth of the perfect morning.

A face rose out of the shadows of his memory and he saw himself as a very young man on another day much like this one and a face that had dimmed with the passing of time into a shadowy image suddenly took form. Painted in colors so vivid and startling that only memory with its nimble fingers can capture.

A little slip of a girl with a big bouquet of wild flowers stood by his side once again. His first bride who had looked so lovely and trusting that day and who had faced life so bravely. A child wife who had been too fragile to bear the demands of a pioneer settler's wife. Like a flower that blooms too early in the spring and is blasted by the cold night wind, so had his young wife succumbed to the rigors of a life that was too harsh for someone as frail and delicate as she had been and who now lay buried beneath the trees on the Fork Mountain Cemetery.

George's fore parents had all married at an early age and he had followed in their foot steps when scarcely more than a lad but death is no respecter of persons. It takes the young as well as the old, so his wife had been snatched away in the prime of her life leaving him alone with small motherless children to raise.[10]

He had looked into her lifeless face, young and unlined as a child's and it had seemed at that time that the storm clouds of life were too thick to ever lift again.

Then somehow as days followed days he found the old saying still to be true "hope springs eternal in the human breast" and so he not only found the clouds of despair lifting but eventually he found the sun also rising in an almost perfect sky and he was able to look to where hope still flourished on the bright horizon.

The sound of horses and wagons and voices brought him back from his reverie and he saw his bride to be in the lead wagon drawn by a pair of dappled gray horses.

People straggled back through the big field. Some on horse back and many more on foot for there had been a mad scrambling from the wagons when they neared the little church leaving only the drivers and a few old folk who had to be assisted from the wagons by the drivers.

It was a time of rejoicing by the whole assemblage, for after the morning service the wedding was to be performed followed by a picnic under the trees along the creek bank.

A Methodist preacher who was holding a stump meeting in the lower section of Little Rock Creek had agreed to perform the ceremony.

As the song of the wind blended with bird song and human voices and leaves slipped from the trees and sailed through the air like colorful elfin clothes blown from an elfin clothes line, George reached up his hand to assist Betsy in alighting from the wagon. While Betsy's brother Moses, who was the driver, hitched up the team, the bride and groom to be disappeared inside the little church that appeared almost dark to them after being in the bright sunlight. The happy crowd after exchanging greetings gathered up children that had scattered like field mice in all directions and followed the happy couple who had preceded them and who now sat waiting on a front row seat which was nothing more than a split log hewn smooth. Compared to standing in the hot sun or drizzling rain, which ever the weather turned out to be, the little log church with its shadowy interior was more than a shelter from the weather, it was a spiritual haven that was to serve the early settlers for many years to come.

---

[10] George is believed to have had 21 children and three wives. One of George Cook's wives was Elizabeth "Betsy" Mckinney, daughter of Dave McKinney. Betsy was George's wife when the 1880 census was taken. They are buried on the Fayette Cook Cemetery. One of his wives was Ebbie McGee.

Shades of Life

Isabel stood once again in the little valley of Dogwood Flats and pondered on the complexity of life. It was late May and already the dogwoods had shed their blooms.

Spring had come early to the mountains and her thoughts turned to her first spring here in John's valley that had been so filled with sweet promise. That brief spring time had held a false promise for her. Even so, when loneliness touched her life to the extent that she had to escape from her every day surroundings she always found refuge in the valley that nestled almost in the shadow of the towering bluff whose scarred old face never changed although it had looked down over the timbered hills at its feet through time immemorial.

Early morning had not separated earth and sky when she had left her bed and stood in the dewy stillness of pre-dawn. She had felt the valley that had shared her joys as well as her sorrows beckoning and long before the sun tipped the summit of Fork Mountain with its fiery glow she was answering the call with eager steps.

As Isabel thought back over the lost years a sadness crept over her being like a cold wind blown from an icy land. She dug her toes into the warm soil beside the rock she was resting on and the earth beneath her bare feet brought a feeling of pleasure. She remembered other mornings when the weather was nippy and how she had made the old cows get up from their resting places and warmed her feet on the ground where they had lain.

The woods surrounding her came alive with song birds and scampering gray squirrels and other small animals of the forest and the tranquility of the early morning setting soon wiped away the sadness. She arose and followed the animal trail she had been traversing until it led out into a small clearing. Here the warm morning sun fell in golden slivers among the yellow dandelions that ran riot in shining clusters along side a spring branch. Isabel got down on her hands and knees to get a drink from the icy water of the bubbling little spring.

She arose and wiped her almost numb lips and chin which had been immerced for a few seconds and shivered when she thought what it would be like to fall head over heels into a chilly flow before the sun had reached its full strength.

Try as she would she could not dispel the thoughts of the past that kept returning to cloud the otherwise perfect morning. She thought about the new grave yard that slashed like an ugly scar across the land where her parents and other members of her family now lay. They who had once been vital human beings were now merging with the soil and she felt at that moment that she too would soon merge with the mother earth and they would become one.

A passage of scripture she had heard her son read from the book of Job came into her mind.

> There the wicked cease from troubling;
> there the weary be at rest.
> There the prisoners rest together;
> they hear not the voice of the oppressor.
> The small and great are there;
> and the servant is free from his master.

During the long months before the birth of her son she had faced up to the harsh realities of life. She had once turned her head when as a young girl she had accompanied the men folk around their trap lines because the killings had made her stomach churn in squeamish rebellion as the helpless animals were clubbed to death.

She had soon learned that there were evils in this new raw land. For a brief period of time she had known life at its best. She still enjoyed the wild beauty that lay within her small world and each season held its own special wonders but she didn't avoid its dark side either.

Even though she abhorred needless cruelty she now had her own trap lines which meant she had to put an end to the suffering animals caught in the cruel steel traps.

The instinct for survival and freedom was a strong force. Here in this section it had produced men with unbounding courage mixed with a deep streak of cruelty. Old mules were loaded beyond their strength then beaten mercilessly when they were unable to move their heavy burdens. Animals were torn to pieces by packs of hunting dogs while men looked on with deep pleasure. Sometimes when the animal proved too game to suit their notion it was shot to slow it up and prolong the fight.

Game cocks were prized possessions and the cruel sport was relished by most of the mountain men. She saw men cut the throats of animals that had been hung from a tree by a chain and gambling stick without the slightest show of compassion for their helpless victims and flay them while they were still kicking.

She also saw those same men with their hard callused hands caring for the sick and helpless as tenderly as a mother would care for her infant. Isabel had learned that black and white were not the only colors in the shades of life. It was interwoven with grays and browns with many colors hard to separate or define.

Characters were molded by the times in which they lived and they were slowly conquering the land. Wild animals had retreated to the roughs and rock cliffs, their final retreat from the hands of men to raise their young and to make their final stand against man who was destined in the future to destroy their last frontier.

Therefore places took on the names of the animals that inhabited them. There was wolf ridge, the bear den and high up on the mountain to the east of Fork Mountain Bluff on the right side of Cook Creek a huge rock cliff jutted out from the face of the mountain like the pouting under lip of a giant and it became known as The Wild Cat Rock. There the big mountain cats found safety in their impenetrable den.

Oft times Isabel had found signs of their bloody kills in the snow during the winter time. She heard the wolves howling on the high ridges but she roamed the mountains unafraid in the company of two huge dogs. Old Nimrod, "so named because he was a fearless hunter" was short of ears and broad of chest. He had inherited all his daring traits from his mixed blooded ancestors.

Goliath, a huge black and yellow tan hound, was bully of the woods with the exception of old Nimrod. With people he was as gentle as a lamb but with the other settlers' dogs it was a different matter, they knew better than to cross him.

Once when she was making the circuit around her trap lines high up on the mountain above Dogwood Flats she paused beside a small stream to rest. Suddenly old Nimrod pricked up his short ears, standing stiff legged, the bristles along his back bone and neck stood up like a porcupine's quills. Then he stuck his tail between his legs and looked toward a rock cliff that jutted from the steep slope on their left. She also looked in that direction and met the yellowish green eyes of the most vicious looking animal she had ever encountered. It was long, slinky and as black as Satan himself.

Paralyzed with fear she stood motionless expecting the evil looking creature to crouch and pounce down on her at any moment.

Suddenly old Nimrod let out a bellowing sound and the echo seemed to bounce from the cliff where the big cat stood motionless except for the tip of its tail which moved back and forth in a serpentine fashion.

At Nimrod's outburst the panther leapt from the cliff and like a streak of black lightening against the white snow it fled up the steep slope and disappeared into the laurel thicket that rimmed the northern tip. Several moments passed as she stood frozen in her tracks. Then from high up on the mountain she heard a blood curdling scream that sounded like a soul in mortal pain and she knew the danger had passed. The panther had headed for the Wild Cat Rock.

Goliath, who had strayed during the encounter with the panther, came racing into view. He sniffed the air then licked Isabel's hand as if in apology for his absence during her time of danger.

Now on this lovely May morning the two dogs squatted on their haunches with tongues dripping and waited with eyes on Isabel's face who was lost in reflection as if reading her every thought as she stood in a burst of golden sun that had found a path through the huge virgin trees that grew all around her.

Nimrod and Goliath were old now. Their muzzles were frosted with white hairs that seemed to be magnified by the discerning brightness. She wondered if the light was as cruel to her as it was to the dogs who had been her constant companions for so many years. She thought of her brother John who had come closer to the fulfillment of his dreams than any of the other settlers who had come to this land of promise, his dream of being a large land owner.

From where she stood she could see the rainbow shaped mountain to the north east of Dogwood Flats high and bluish against the clear sky. Her brother's boundary line reached to the balsams on the slopes of Roan Mountain.

For a moment she closed her eyes and wondered where the years had gone. Then coming back to the present she shaded her vision with her hand against the glare of the warm sun. She looked southward to the high peak to the right of the gap which now bore the name of Pumpkin Patch Mountain.

The picture in her mind was as vivid and clear as it had been on that first day when she stood on the brow of that mountain as a fourteen year old girl and viewed the land that was so filled with beauty and promise.

Isabel allowed her gaze to wander to the high peaks to the left of the gap to where only a short time ago they had loomed dark and slate gray against a wintry sky but today they stood majestic in the early morning mist. Spring had clothed them to perfection and as the gentle wind moved across the face of the mountain they glowed in iridescent splendor.

Isabel had no particular destination in mind. She was out to enjoy the day but soon she found herself on an old familiar path that would eventually lead into a clearing where the sounds of children playing and splashing in the shallows of a brisk mountain stream could be heard. Children whose happy voices blended with the songs of the cat-birds in the cherry and apple trees. A place where the blue smoke would be curling up from a cabin where the morning meal was being prepared.

The past was a sad dim shadow that would follow her always, the future was unknown and uncertain. The here and now was all that mattered. She was almost smothered by the here and now as the cries of "Grandma!" greeted her and a flock of children of all sizes flitted around her like colorful butterflies. Small chubby hands clung to her long skirt while the older ones kissed her soundly on her cheeks and hugged her with cold arms that were still wet from the branch water.

Young fingers entwined with hers, pulling her toward the open cabin door where the delicious aroma of cooking food greeted her, making her mouth water.

Home is where the heart is and this valley was her heart's home and the children, the birds and everything seemed to be rejoicing that she had come.

The Lost Silver Mine

Since coming to this valley John had spent precious little time for his own pleasure. His every waking hour had been devoted to building up his homestead and working so he could accumulate more acreage.

At first when his children were small the going had been rough and he was very much tied to the land but as his family grew he found more and more time to work on a job that paid ten cents a day. Land could be bought for five cents an acre and John never spent his hard earned money for anything but land. The farm supported them and now he owned acres and acres his feet had never touched.

So he decided it was time for him to take off a day now and then from his daily routine and explore his vast holdings. Of all the property he owned, the high mountain that bordered the southern portion was his favorite. There was something about its lofty height and deep hollows that seemed to draw him like a magnet.

By this time in his life, John had grown sons but none of them cared to help their father explore the wild terrain. The virgin timber on the mountain slopes was so large and thick their branches formed a canopy over head and it was hard for the explorer to keep his bearings.

It was a twilight world that was kind of spooky even to a seasoned veteran of the mountains such as he. A place where panthers could spring from one of the huge overhead branches at any time. A place with laurel thickets on the ridges that were dense where bears could be near yet hidden from view.

On one such excursion John had glimpsed a dark shadow at the base of a rock cliff. As he peered into the gloom he heard a strange slapping sound then he discovered it was a huge black bear slapping a fallen log with its paw, warning him to come no closer.

He had slowly backed away until he had put a safe distance between himself and the bear. Then he turned tail and fled down the steep mountain side. He decided at that time he had done enough exploring for one day.

Each day of exploring brought a new adventure in one form or another. Some days the forest was alive with sounds of all kinds and on others it was as quiet as the grave, days when he felt he was traveling in a world where time had no meaning. Even the birds were quiet among the timber where the ringing of an axe had never been heard, a world as untouched by the hand of man as the garden of Eden before man was created.

John knew if he should loose his way while rambling around and become confused in the deep shadows all he had to do was follow one of the streams down to where Little Rock Creek flowed at the base of the mountain. Almost every hollow had its own stream, water trickled down the face of rock cliffs for the timber afforded a perfect water shed.

John stopped by the side of a brisk little stream that fell from the cliffs above. It bubbled and murmured in a sheltered little cove above a place where the land fell steeply away a few hundred yards below, forming a trough like hollow with steep slopes on either side.

The hollow was so steep and narrow one would have to hold to shrubs and tree branches to descend into its dimness.

Before drinking from the cold mountain stream John paused and took a closer look at his surroundings. Toward the southern rim ferns grew between cracks in the rock cliffs and green beds of mosses formed a thick carpet beneath his feet. A giant black gum tree, old and gnarled, grew on the opposite side of the stream and leaned twisted and bent at a northerly slant. Its huge branches spread high overhead in all four directions.

As John lay down to drink, a streak of bright sunlight fell on the water. Perhaps the wind as it traveled across the face of the mountain had parted the foliage overhead allowing the sun beam to penetrate the shadowy cove. What ever the cause, as John's face came near the water the sun beam struck some kind of substance that gleamed like a silver dollar in the stream.

His thirst forgotten, John rose to his feet and felt for his hunting knife which he carried on his belt. Kneeling down he jabbed with the point of his knife and found the shinny metal soft enough so he could gouge chunks of it loose with the knife blade.

After gouging several chunks of the metal loose he dropped it into his haber sack and then he carefully covered the exposed substance with flat rocks from the stream bed.

Whatever the shiny mineral was, he had apparently struck a pure vein. John knew there were other secrets buried on the mountain. Little golden flakes washed out of the earth and was carried by the streams. It glittered in the sand and on leaves beside the streams where the water splattered down their rocky course.

Before leaving the little cove John carved a big cross-mark on the huge black gum tree, then slowly made his way down the mountain being careful to fix land marks in his mind so he could return to that particular spot any time he desired to do so.

The finding of the mineral became a carefully guarded secret. John knew if outsiders were to find out about the mineral he had discovered it would bring undesirable fortune hunters to his valley and although several of the family clan had come to his valley by this time and settled they were still comparatively few in number if trouble over a mine should arise.

John melted the mineral he had found and ran bullets for his gun. Some of the family members were inclined to believe it was lead, while others argued that lead was a bluish color, not shiny like the stuff John had found.

One day an outsider, who happened to ride into the valley, discovered the kind of bullets John was using quite by accident. "Where on earth did you get the silver for your bullets?," he asked in amazement. "That's not silver, hit's lead", he replied and hastily changed the subject.

The stranger brought the conversation back to the bullets again, "I've worked in a silver mine and that bullet is pure silver. Silver is whiter than lead and has a luster that lead don't have."

For many months after the conversation with the stranger John carried an uneasy feeling in the pit of his stomach. What if the news got out about the silver bullet? But apparently the man had sensed John's desire for secrecy and had kept his mouth shut.

John never talked about the location of the silver except to his wife. He asked her to accompany him to the location but she declined. She had no desire to traverse the rough terrain that was the habitat of bears and other wild animals and besides she was not as spry as she once had been.

In his old age John passed on the information about the cross he had cut on the big black gum tree but that was the extent of his revelation and the secret of the silver went to the grave with him.

After crossing the old boundary line and traversing only a short distance on the southern side of John's mountain one can see the wisdom the old man used when he decided to keep his side of the mountain intact, old mine shafts, dangerous and uncovered, yawns a treacherous death trap to the unwary.

The scars on that side of the mountain will mar its beauty as long as the mountain exists. On Lick Ridge, "so named because of a natural deposit of salt rock where deer and other animals in the long ago days of yesteryear came to lick," was where the main mine was located. From this vantage point one can look down on McKinney Cove.

After the mine closed down the deep chasm gaped open in the side of the ridge, a very real danger for adventuresome kids who often prowled around the old mine site.

Several years after the mine had been abandoned the cavity caved in causing houses to quiver and windows to rattle on both sides of the mountain. But on the north side there is still no mine holes. The timber has been cut over and fields have been cleared on its rugged old slopes but it is still a place of wild beauty. A place where all kinds of herbs can be found, a place where a cold stream still trickles down from the rock cliffs and it's still a place where hopeful hearts of different ages still look closely as they cross the mountain streams thinking that perhaps they too may catch a glimpse of something shiny in the water as John did in the days of long ago.

Lost Paradise

The residents of Little Rock Creek had come a long way since the long ago day when John walked through the gap in the mountain for the first time.

The northern half of the mountain known as John's mountain, as seen from Dogwood Flats, lies steep and rugged. Its boundary line skips along the very top, so trees silhouetted against the sky on the southeastern section of Hopson[11] property. The boundary line on Hopson's mountain reached the balsams on the slopes of Roan Mountain. The wish that had been only a dream when John Hopson first came to the Little Rock Creek section was now a reality. Now he was the only owner of huge land holdings. His property laid from the slopes of the northern mountain to the top of the southern mountain with vast acreage in between.

At first John had considered a land grant and he was told in order to get the desired acreage he would have to call it a ranch. Under that title he could obtain a thousand acres and he was advised to do so and use slave labor. The idea of slavery rankled in his mind. Also, he knew the other settlers' views on the subject of colored slaves. So the outcome was he purchased nine hundred sixty three acres at twenty five cents an acre. He also owned more than three hundred acres on the headwaters of Green Creek which he bought from a man named Avery.

Most of the settlers like John had prospered immensely since their humble beginnings.

Homesteads had taken on the look of permanency, many of the pole cabins had been replaced with well built hewn log houses, strong log barns and granaries and smoke houses bespoke of thrift and prosperity. Cattle roamed at will through the mountains and herds increased despite the wild animals that still preyed on them. Corn cribs bulged with corn from the rich new grounds that were being cleared year by year. Worm fences crawled up, down and around the mountain fields.

The glad young land with its sparkling streams and deep woodlands offered everything a freedom loving soul could ever ask for. Tranquility reigned in this little mountain pocket where life was simple and good.

The ominous clouds of war were fast gathering on the horizon but here in the mountains, shut away from the outside world time passed unhurriedly on gossamer wings.

Their awakening from their Utopian dreams into a nightmarish world of plundering and death made the road ahead seem very dark and frightening. The news spread that the country was tottering on the brink of war, then like a dark mist carried over the mountains by an evil wind the news came that civil war was not just a threat but a stark reality.

Brave men shook in their boots, never-the-less, they kissed their families goodbye and marched away. Many never to return to their native hills.

Fear of starvation gripped the people who were left. One crop failure could mean going hungry. One thing was in their favor, the mountains were alive with wild game but with the able bodied men away at war who would bring the meat to their pots?

Evil yawned like a spiritual Charybdis threatening to suck them down into its chilling depths forever.

---

[11] First records show the name was Hobson and was later changed to Hopson.

The Capture

It was a beautiful day in mid-June. The birds sang in the young cherry trees and over on the laurel hill to the west of Dogwood Flats a chicken hawk whistled from its perch on a dead limb in a gnarled old chestnut tree. Its keen eyes scanned the terrain from the lofty height of the steep ridge.

Jane Cook stood beneath an early June apple tree that her father George Cook had grafted. This was its first season of bearing and the young fruit was turning a pinkish red, like the blush on the cheeks of a healthy mountain girl.

As she stood in the tree's cool shade she could see her father pacing slowly back and forth across the yard where the ground was worn bare by the many feet that had left their foot prints throughout the years.

The yard was hard packed and had to be swept with a broom. Flower beds like tiny oasises in a miniature desert rose in mounds, wisteria twined and wrapped around banister posts and rambling roses grew in tangled masses along the picket fence that separated the yard from the garden.

As Jane looked at her father's bowed head and slumped shoulders her heart was filled with a surge of rage. Her older brother was away at war and her father, like the rest of the family was deeply concerned for his safety. Most of the able bodied men were gone and the shock of war had thrown the residents of Little Rock Creek into a state of panic and despair.

On the surface the day was filled with promise beneath a blue cloudless sky but the storm clouds of war first hand was to sweep down over Dogwood Flats for the first time on that near perfect day in the form of Confederate soldiers, who had left the main road that led toward Roan Valley and rode up the old sled road on the left of Cook Creek.

Stopping at the old Presswood place the soldiers ransacked the house and terrorized the occupants. Leaving the Presswood premises they turned west and entered Dogwood Flats at the head of the valley.

William "Bill" Cook was only a boy barely in his teens. War to him was just something the old folks talked about, romanticized in his young mind by brave heroic visions of young men in uniforms and of far away battle fields. He had often visualized himself astride a fine horse, bigger than life, the possessor of unearthly strength.

His fancy often carried him through enemy lines and over obstacles that would have stopped ordinary men. He heard the whine of bullets as they passed so close he felt his skin burn but never a scratch did he get nor a drop of blood did he loose.

The roar of the cannons meant nothing to him. His horse's mane that blew in the wind was always smooth and untangled and shone like polished brass as he rode for endless miles without feeling the strain of hardships.

But that day in June destroyed forever any illusions of grandiosity he had ever possessed. Bill was to learn in the bitter months ahead that instead of beautiful horses with flowing manes he would see bony mules caked with filth and blood pried from the frozen ground because they were too weak and sick to get up on their own strength and instead of riding he would walk seemingly endless miles hungry and thirsty chained to other men, driven like animals to the slaughter.

So in his innocence on that fateful day instead of running he had gawked at the soldiers in his surprise. By the time he realized his predicament it was too late. He found himself surrounded and presently chained to several other men who wore a dazed expression on their bruised faces. Bill looked at the soldier in command as he set astride a big dappled gray horse. The man looked more brutish than the horse he was riding because his florid face, frizzy side burns and paunchy stomach gave him a swinish appearance.

The man chained next to Bill started to whisper something to him but the commanding officer suddenly spurred his mount. As he passed the man who had spoken to Bill he gave a vicious kick meant for the face and luckily the man lowered his head in that instant and the toe of his boot struck his scalp just above the hair line.

Bill felt as if he himself had received the blow. He stared in horror as a big bluish lump popped up almost egg sized on the man's head. Blood, thin and watery, like drops of sweat clung to the hairs, then slipped as if greased through the hair line leaving bloody streaks on his right cheek.

Youth's young spirit that had flown so lightly during Bill's short life span now lay prostrate. It would never soar again for its gossamer wings had been torn to threads before man's inhumanity to man.

As Jane stood beneath the apple tree watching a robin feeding its young she heard the sound of hoof-beats. Looking toward the wagon road she saw a band of soldiers approaching and they were dressed in the gray of the Confederacy along with a group of men who walked in a strange hobbling fashion. Fright seemed to lend wings to her feet as she scurried across the short distance that separated her from the house.

Apparently the family had heard the hoof-beats for they hastily gathered in the yard as she closed the gap between them. Breathless, she stood shaking with an unknown terror as the soldiers approached.

In the yard a rooster of undeterminable breed crowed loudly, then started scratching while hens crowded and vied for the worms he dug up in the edge of a blossom bed. The soldiers rode up in the yard unmindful of the flowers they trampled. Dismounting, they tied the horses to the porch banisters then swarmed all over the place.

Suddenly Jane glanced at the line of men who had walked so strangely when she first saw them. They had stopped several yards behind the soldiers who had blocked them from view when they were mounted. Now she understood and almost fainted when she saw her brother Bill among the prisoners. The look of distress on his young face made her throw all caution to the wind. She flew at the soldier who stood nearest the prisoners with his lips curled in a smile of contempt as he dodged her flailing fists and sharp finger nails.

But the commanding officer failed to be amused. As she screamed and clawed he caught her arm from behind and jerked her around violently, then shook her until her teeth rattled.

When her head cleared from the shaking he had given her, she found her face only inches away from his. She looked directly into his cruel eyes but she could not tell the color for they reflected the verdurous surroundings.

He gave her a shove that sent her sprawling into one of the flower beds. It so happened it was the one where the rooster was feeding his hens. Her sudden landing amid his juicy worms startled the rooster beyond measure. He bounced up in the air like a rubber ball and the hens scattered.

When the rooster landed near her with his ruffled feathers looking very much like a gigantic fuzz ball he arched his neck and let out a sound more like a scream than a cackle. His little reddish eyes held a stormy look as if telling her through the language of eye contact that he would give her a good flogging if she ever dared to bother his diggings again.

The soldiers who had witnessed the proceedings guffawed loudly. One of them approached her and bowed grandly, "your highness, could I offer you a hand?" Humiliated and angry she scrambled to her feet ready to do battle again but the officer who had shoved her down blocked her path. His little pig-like eyes narrowed to slits as he asked her bluntly, "lady are you going to shut up, or will I have to set this building on fire and burn it down around you?" Jane knew she was treading on dangerous ground and that she could bring disaster to the rest of the family. She bit her lips and shed tears of anger and frustration as the officer shoved her aside and swaggered over to where the prisoners stood chained and miserable. He heaped foul and abusive language on his helpless victims who stood with down cast eyes and bruised faces.

Old Gabriel, the family dog, a cross bred and fiercely loyal to the family showed his teeth and growled low in his throat as the officer began to make fun of Bill and slap him around. Old Gabriel squatted to spring but one of the soldiers raised his foot and gave the dog a vicious kick in the ribs that raised him off the ground. He landed in a heap with all the wind knocked from his lungs. Finally the dog coughed in a dry croupy manner then tucking his tail between his legs he slunk away, his pride like Jane's had reached its lowest ebb.

Later, after the soldiers had departed Jane wondered in a numb detached way why she had reacted the way she had to the day's events? Even the incident with the rooster had seemed humorous amid the collapse of her and the family's world.

She had lain in the flower bed and almost giggled at the indignant look of the rooster who was now, along with most of his hens, being digested in the hated rebels stomachs.

How could she see humor in any situation when her brother, young and defenseless, stood bound in chains and her father, old and heart sick, seeming to age before her very eyes? How could her mind be on other things when she had witnessed the ending of the world she had always known?

Now standing alone in the dewy dampness of the evening just before deep twilight spread its dusty blanket over the land, she looked at the trampled flowers and chicken feathers. She looked at her father as he sat on the porch. Even the darkening shadows could not hide the dejection that showed even in his very posture.

A deep hatred flared up like a flame within her being that was to smolder until the day she died. Sorrow, deep as the dark hollows between steep mountains engulfed her at that moment. It washed over her like the waves of a tossing sea, lashing and tearing her apart. It met and mingled with the fire of hatred and helplessness until she rolled on the ground screaming, laughing and moaning.

As the emotional storm roared through her being she was engulfed in an ocean of oblivion. Darkness fell over the mountains and the moon sailed high in the heavens, wearing a shroud of mist that hid its face from the troubled world below.

The long cruel march began to the Confederate prison somewhere below the mountains, Bill had no idea where, for he had never been very far from his native hills.

He had crossed the mountains to the north of Dogwood Flats several times to visit kin folks in Tennessee but the direction they had taken that fateful day was a trail he had never trodden before which led southward.

The whole journey was like a nightmarish dream. Thirst, weariness and hunger stalked their every step and continued to follow like a specter throughout the seemingly endless days and nights after reaching their destination.

The misery, filth and suffering was more than his young mind could comprehend. He had to hold his nose against the stench of putrid flesh and of unsanitary conditions that were beyond description. He tried to close his eyes against the moans of the dying and the screams of the wounded but they were scenes and sounds that would be stamped indelibility on his mind throughout the remainder of his short life span.

During the day the able bodied prisoners were forced to work under the watchful eyes of armed guards. At night they lay on filthy straw on the floor. Steel bands encircled their wrists and the chains that bound them were embedded in the walls.

For Bill time ceased to be counted in days, weeks and months. It merged into an eternal passage in an infernal region beyond any depths of human reason.

Oft times as he lay hungry and exhausted between other prisoners his mind took flight and swung back and forth from reality to fancy like the pendulum of the old eight day clock that stood on the mantel in the hours where he had spent most of his days.

He felt such joy as his mind soared across the high mountains where it always came to rest in the little hidden valley of Dogwood Flats. He could see and hear the sights and sounds almost as clear as if he were actually there.

The leaving of the cows at the milk gap in late afternoon around the time when the sun dropped behind Lonnie's Knob in a splash of glory, turning the high mountain tops into a scene of burnished splendor.

He could see the old people setting on the porches or on steps, resting their weary bones after a long day of puttering around the homesteads. He could hear children who gathered in the early twilight in gangs to play the old mountain games. He could smell the scents on the soft evening breezes.

In his dreams everything was divided in two parts. It was pure heaven when his spirit came to rest in his childhood home among the high mountains but when the pendulum of time swung in the other direction hell lay before him yawning and uncovered.

In his inert condition he was ill prepared for what followed. One morning after a night of restless dreams, he seemed to be floating through a mist of unbearable misery when suddenly he was literally raised off the floor by a kick planted firmly on his rear-end. Pain like a blaze of fire shot through his body. One of the stronger prisoners who was chained next to Bill helped him to his feet. Sleep fled like shadows from the noon day sun but his vision was still blurred as they stepped outside to face a bright cloudless morning.

Bill rubbed his eyes and staggered on wobbly legs trying to get his bearings and almost collided with the same mean tempered officer who had captured him in the beginning.

The Confederate officer surveyed the bedraggled crew of prisoners from head to toe, "Now then!" he exclaimed in a loud mocking tone. "You fellas sure are a sight for sore eyes". Then placing both hands on his bulging hips he began to strut around like a fat turkey gobbler. "I guess you think you've got it made, living here in the lap of luxury while others fight the war fer you." At his words the guards sniggered, "Well, you all have another thought coming!"

With that he paused and pushed his big face forward, his fat jowls shaking like a fattening hog. Bill shrank from his gimlet-eyed stare. He recalled the needless abuse he had heaped on all the men the day they were taken prisoner and at that time his spirit had been crushed like a fledgling that had fluttered from its nest and was too young to fly. Now he feared his physical being was in danger of being crushed as well.

But the officer had other plans in mind, while they ate their measly morning meal he explained in grisly details what lay in store for them. The crux of the matter was this. They, the prisoners, who were trapped like animals, were going to march before the rebel soldiers unarmed and wearing Confederate uniforms.

"You fellas are going to face your own kind. We'll see how you like that with us behind and the blue bellies in front. You birds will be caught in the cross fire!" Faces paled at the words of the Confederate officer. They knew they would be marching straight into the jaws of death!

The officer squinted his little evil eyes that were almost hidden in his fat face against the morning light. The beauty of the early sun drenched world was lost to his vision. His only aim was to degrade and humiliate his helpless victims.

After giving orders for the prisoners to stay close together and to march straight ahead, he mounted his horse and the procession started out through the open country.

The prisoners were hard pressed to keep ahead of the mounted soldiers but the instinct for self preservation will struggle in the human breast until the last hope fades.

Off in the far distance Bill could see a growth of large timber cutting across the open land but he knew his legs would never carry him that far in his weakened condition. Just as he was about to sink to the ground the officer called a halt.

The ground on which the prisoners sprawled didn't look very fertile. Patches of broom sage ripped in the breezes that blew, soft as angel breath, across the wide expanse and Bill felt a pang of home sickness when he thought of the rich black soil of his native mountains.

The rest was brief but it gave the prisoners strength to rise and try again. The lay of the land made the distance deceiving and an undeterminable amount of time passed before reaching the timber that loomed dark and forbidding against the eastern horizon and Bill wondered what evil lurked in the shadows beneath the spreading branches.

The trail through the timber was narrow, so much so, the soldiers rode single file. Two of them were ordered to dismount and walk with the prisoners in case any of them should take it into their heads to try to escape.

Their horses were tied behind the soldier bringing up the rear.

Temptation, sweet and brief as a maiden's smile flashed through the heart of each of the prisoners here in this wooded area. With huge trees to dodge between it was the ideal place to bound and run but with the officer riding in front of them with a rifle he could raise and fire almost instantly and two armed soldiers walking with them, hope flickered and died like a candle carried outside in a blustering wind.

Everything in the forest was quiet and still. Not even a bird twittered in the trees and the heavy ground covering from last fall's leaves muffled the clop clop of the horses hoofs.

At last a halt was called and Bill found himself standing in a small clearing which some how seemed odd, being completed surrounded on all sides by the virgin forest.

It was apparent the trees had been cleared away in the long ago past. No rotting logs or stumps cluttered the place. Deer and other wild animals had kept it picked clean. The one odd feature in this strange setting was a vine covered object that protruded from the level floor of the clearing.

The Confederate soldiers tied their horses in the thick timber well out of sight above the beaten path. Drawn by the vine covered mound one of the soldiers decided to take a closer look. He opened a pocket knife and began to cut and saw at the tangled vines. Another curious soldier joined in and soon the vines gave way as the soldiers pulled and tugged, breaking the vine's tenacious hold.

It was a strange moment! Soldiers and captains alike gathered close to watch the proceedings. War, death and suffering were blotted out temporarily from their tired minds and a moment of comradliness, like a fresh breeze, took their place.

To all their surprise and delight, the mouth of an old fireplace was revealed. The soldiers crowded around, shaking their heads in wonder, "imagine," one of the soldiers spoke softly, " a house once stood here in this clearing! I can almost smell the good bread that once browned in an old oven in embers on this hearth-stone.

"Where are the rest of the chimney stones? There's not a loose stone in this whole clearing." The soldiers were all chattering away, expressing their own individual opinions. "Hauled away. Haven't you noticed the scarcity of stones in this section?" "Well, I hadn't thought of that. Guess they do gather every stone they can find to re-use after all this old fireplace has long ago done its due."

"Alright, this ain't no social gathering!" the mood was instantly broken but Bill had observed the commanding officer's face when the fireplace was first discovered and the far-away wishful expression on his face when they talked about the smell of baking bread and faces from long ago.

Their next stop was at the eastern edge of the forest. They had left the horses and proceeded on foot and Bill could see a large field running north and south as he peered through the timber. Then the commanding officer began speaking, " see that low lying ridge across that field? We're going across the timbered spot to where them Yankees are camped just beyond in a field."

When the officer spoke again a worried frown appeared between his eyes, "speaking of the scout, he was to be waiting here. He said there was just a small group of them and in his opinion they were sitting around waiting for reinforcements. "Now", the officer spoke in his old familiar aggressive tone. As he strode back and forth in front of the men, his pompous manner was almost comical. He looked for the world like a big fat defeathered bird with his big protrusive belly bulging out above the tight trousers of his uniform.

He stopped his strutting stride for a moment and fixed his little beady eyes on the captives. "Maybe we can even strike up a bargain with them mangy coyotes. Their surrender for the likes of this motley crew. Although", with that he paused and looked at the prisoners with utter most contempt, "Why anyone would give a plugged nickel for the whole lot of ya'll is beyond me!"

It was plain to see as the minutes dragged on that the officer was worried. Finally he voiced his uneasiness, "The scout was supposed to meet us here in this wooded area. Something has caused his delay." The day was waning. Soon it would be too late to carry out their plans and the success of their mission depended on the daylight.

After what seemed an hour, in reality it had only been a few minutes, the officer barked a command. The soldiers responded instantly and almost before the prisoners knew what was happening they found themselves marching before the soldiers through the open field at the edge of the forest.

Soldiers and captives alike were jumpy with nerves as taunt as banjo strings. They had reached the middle of the field when someone stepped on a dry limb that had blown from the woods they had just vacated. In the quietness the sound of the snapping limb carried loud as a pistol shot. Suddenly one of the prisoners panicked and bolted. Like a match touched to fuel, panic spread like wild fire. The prisoners scattered through the field like frightened animals.

The field in which the prisoners and soldiers were crossing was an over grown pasture that had been farmed in times past. An old fence line wrapped in honey suckle vines ran between the field and the low timbered ridge. Union soldiers who had been hiding behind the vine covered fence rose simultaneously and began firing at the Confederate soldiers, little dreaming that many of the men facing them were in reality prisoners of the Confederate army.

The Rebels had set a trap and fallen there-in. For at the first gun shot, Union soldiers seemed to materialize from behind every tree and fallen log on the low lying ridge directly to the east.

A voice from somewhere yelled "charge", a bugle sounded, mingled with the screams of wounded men and heavy gun fire.

When pandemonium broke loose in the field Bill had no time to think. His legs were the only thing that worked, so he ran blindly in whatever direction they carried him. Up ahead to his right he saw a stagnant pool. Cattails grew thick along its banks and he headed toward the pool intending to skirt its northern rim and head for a pine thicket that grew at the base of the low ridge farther south.

A huge weeping willow tree grew between him and the pool. As he ran head long he heard the whine of bullets close to his head and a thud as they buried deep into the willow.

At this juncture in time Bill seemed to be out of his body and floating, light as thistle down in the air over the field, while his body was earth bound and running like crazy.

In this strange state he saw the Confederate officer up ahead leaping at high speed through the coarse brown grass and dead weeds that had dried during last winter's cold and strange as it may seem in those critical moments, he observed the new blades of grass mingled with the old growth.

Somehow Bill knew the officer was heading for the same pine thicket. He also knew if they both made it across the open space death would be waiting for him in the form of a Confederate bullet.

Bill saw the officer stop suddenly on the rim of the pool, then straighten up as straight as an arrow, then topple and fall with a loud splash into the slimy water.

Bill gathered his strength and put all he could muster into his next leap. At the instant his feet touched the grass it was as if the earth fell away from beneath his feet.

The Escape

After the great leap which took all his strength, he found himself lying on the ground in what seemed to be a deep ditch. He lay there stunned and bewildered and he wondered if a bullet had found its mark and had numbed him, for he felt no pain.

Maybe he was already dead and in the grave. As he felt the dirt beneath his fingers his head jerked up in a startled motion and all he could see above him was thick brown grass with a splashing of blue sky here and there between the grass blades.

He dropped his head down on his arms and tried to reason. His thoughts were jumbled but he knew then he was not dead, or even wounded. He must have landed in a deep narrow gully and the long matted grass that grew around its edges had closed over him again.

Gun fire sounded around him and he knew men were dying but he lay face down in his small sanctuary as the sounds slowly receded. He was a boy again, playing among the old fields of Dogwood Flats in all of youth's sweet innocence. The sound of gun fire became the sounds of pop guns loaded with green haws and the screams of wounded men became the laughing voices of childhood comrades.

Time passed, whether minutes or hours he could not tell. Once when his mind cleared for a second, he heard only sporadic gun fire, then silence. His underground haven cradled him in its comforting embrace and he slept in dreamless sleep.

Night settled over the land and a great golden moon sailed overhead when Bill finally awoke alert and refreshed. Like a butterfly emerging from its cocoon, he cautiously rose to his feet and felt the coarse grass scrape his face as his head cleared the underground burrow.

The huge weeping willow tree whose shadow fell black as ebony in contrast with the simmering moon glow moved with motions when the wind stirred its branches like a giant pre-historic monster.

The pool, now a dark hole in the earth, lay still and silvery in the center due to the moon's reflection. He thought of his tormentor now lying at the bottom of the pool and shuddered.

To the north a deep forest, a pastel yellowish green in the daylight due to its tender budding, now lay black as if chiseled in stone as it rose in crooked outline against the night sky. Like a frightened rabbit he scurried for the black circle beneath the willow and stood holding his breath while his eyes searched the moon drenched terrain for movements or sounds. He half expected Rebel soldiers to spring at him from all directions but nothing moved in the ghostly silence and he finally took heart and moved from the sheltering shadows.

Only a short time had passed since men were fighting and dying in this now silent field and it was an eerie place to be. Even the trees looked shrouded and ghostly as the wind that had suddenly risen, breaking the stillness, shook their branches which seemed to be pointing long accusing skeleton like fingers in his direction and in fancy it seemed they were moving ever closer.

And the voice of the whispering trees seemed to be asking why he was the only living human there in that field of death. Fright gave him strength he didn't know he possessed and he fled like a shadow blown by the wind northward toward the black forbidding forest which could offer him shelter or swallow him up forever amid the evil that could easily lurk beneath its twisted branches.

Hunger, like a twisting serpent, squirmed within Bill's stomach for what seemed like an endless time, then the gnawing pain stopped and a weakness that made him feel lightheaded took its place.

He kept within the shadowy shelter of the forest during the day. Skirting near the edge now and then but never daring to venture out into the open. He watched the sunrise in the mornings and sunset in the evenings so he could get his bearings. The sun was his only guide and he was careful to note its disappearing like a fiery ball beyond the far horizon.

At last, too weak and tired to walk any farther he sat in the edge of the forest and observed a homestead below. He saw a woman and two children working around the place but they were the only signs of life. No dog barked and no rooster crowed to greet the coming day.

Bill knew he had to do something or literally starve to death. So just as objects began to take shape in the early dawn he left the woods and walked nearer to the house and hid in a pine thicket that hovered like a setting hen in an old cow pasture. He not only needed food, he was also out of water and desperation drove him to drastic measures. Maybe the lady of the house would take pity on him and give him water to drink and food to eat. Then again, she might shoot him on sight, any way, he had to take the chance.

The sun had spread, like a golden blanket, over the land when he saw the woman and two children emerge from the house. They went to an out building and got some tools and started westward across the fields. This was the chance he had been waiting for. He left the pine thicket and walked as fast as his weak legs could carry him to the house.

The building was fairly large. First he made sure no one else was there before going to the kitchen. A tea kettle suspended on a wire over the embers simmered, making a cheerful sound as the steam escaped from its spout. A large iron pot sat on the hearth-stone and when he lifted the lid he discovered it was filled with large grains of hominy.

A wave of home sickness washed through his being, making him physically ill. The cheery warmth of the kitchen, the singing tea kettle and the pot of hominy. He squatted down by the fireplace and wept like a small child.

When the over powering wave of emotion subsided, he rose and went to the cupboard finding a dish and spoon. He dipped out a heaping mound of the hominy and fought the temptation to cram his mouth full of the delicious food because he knew if he didn't take his time his stomach would reject it.

So he started out grain by grain. He chewed it carefully and gradually built up to a normal bite. The feeling was heavenly. Warmth built up in his stomach and flowed through his being. He stopped and drank from the water bucket that sat on a small kitchen table, then returned to finish the rest of the hominy in the bowl.

Bill was tempted to take more of the hominy for a future meal, then he thought of the woman and children digging in the field. No doubt planting a garden that could not be seen from the house in case of raiders.

He poured out some hot water and washed the bowl and spoon and put them in their proper place in the cupboard. He drank again, deeply this time for the hominy had made him thirsty. Next, he went into the down stairs bedroom looking for something to put on for at present he looked like a scare crow that had come alive and had just walked out of a corn patch. The Confederate uniform he had been forced to wear was dirty and hung from his bony frame as shapeless as if it hung on a clothes rack.

He found nothing in the bedrooms but women and children's clothing. He started to go up to the second floor when he noticed a closet door beneath the stairs. He opened the door and found it contained men's clothing. It was apparent the man of the house was either away or dead.

The clothes had been ironed with utmost care with the dress clothes hanging in front. Bill's eyes traveled down the line until he found a pair of work trousers and shirt. After carefully folding them he closed the closet door.

He hoped as he left the premises that the woman would not miss the clothing or the hominy. He had never felt so guilty about anything in his young life and he carried his head high to keep from looking at the pants and shirt.

The Homeward Journey

Later on in the day he crossed a small stream that flowed lazily through the flat land. He rolled up his trousers and waded upstream until he found a secluded spot hidden away in a willow patch. Stripping off the filthy clothes he was wearing he sat down in the water and washed to this heart's content. If only he had some soap but he was thankful for the stream and he had sand with which to scrub his scaly feet and hands.

But his hair was another matter. It was long and matted and tangled. He could not get it completely clean without soap due to the oil that clung stubbornly to every strand but the handfuls of sand he rubbed into his scalp helped immensely so that with the final rinse the strands separated and blew softly in the warm breeze.

Before leaving the peaceful seclusion of the willows where he had been able to completely relax for the first time since he had been taken captive, Bill rolled the hated Rebel uniform up in a tight bundle and buried it in the mud near the stream.

Late that afternoon he chanced upon a terrible scene. The homestead that had only recently stood there lay in ashes along with all the out buildings. Two blackened chimneys stood tall and forlorn looking, as if bewildered. What had happened here only they had witnessed. Now they stood in stately silence, keeping their secrets forever locked within their stony hearts.

Bill wondered if the utter destruction had been caused by soldiers or raiders. He walked by the charred remains and on through the greening fields where dandelions nodded in the passing breeze and to his surprise he came upon a barn hidden away by a low rounded knoll that was timbered in pine.

Bill knew who ever had destroyed the other buildings had struck from a different direction, otherwise this building would now lay in ashes also. He moved with hesitant steps toward the well built barn whose door was closed and slowly raised the latch. The gloom in the barn after being out in the bright sunlight took some time for his eyes to adjust, then he saw he had stepped into a long hall. Walking down the shadowy interior he counted three stalls on the right. Part of the long hall had been boxed and a door, also shut, was placed in the center. Bill opened each stall door and looked in. It was possible that an animal could be trapped inside but he found them all empty.

He opened the hall door and stepped in. It was a tack-room. A ladder led up into the loft and a saddle hung on the wall along with a bridle and saddle blanket. All kinds of paraphernalia needed on a farm was stored in the room and from a peg in the wall a heavy work coat was hanging as if it had been hung there only that day. He took it down and tried it on and he was almost lost in its comforting folds.

Bill thought of the journey ahead. He knew when he reached the foot-hills the nights would be chilly. He folded the coat as tight as he could, then wrapped it in the saddle blanket and tied it with rawhide throngs that also swung from a peg. He tied several of the throngs to the bundle so he could make a back pack.

He carried the bundle up the ladder and found the loft to be half full of straw and hay. He was hungry and wondered where his next meal would come from. He stretched out in the clean straw and laid his head on the bundle he had made. "Just fer awhile", he told himself. He intended to explore some more before night fall but night fell and the moon rose bright and golden and crossed the heavens and sank out of sight in the west and Bill slept on. He had a clean bed and clean clothes. What more could a weary soul ask for amid a world torn apart by a savage senseless civil war?

Bill woke next morning feeling refreshed. He looked up at the shadowy ceiling of the barn with a bewildered feeling. He lay quietly until memory flooded back to the time he had lain down to rest on the straw. The gloom in the barn loft made it impossible to guess the time of day so he rose and picked up the bundle he had used for a pillow and climbed down the ladder.

As he stood at the landing he observed several things that had escaped his attention on entering the tack room the first time. A huge pair of antlers spread wide up near the top of the southern wall and a canvas haversack and canteen swung below them. Bill knew who ever had owned this place had loved to hunt.

He reached up an took the haversack down from the wall. Inside he found a flint on a piece of steel along with several other items needed for camping, one of which was a large pocket knife. Bill stood lost in thought. Sometimes strangers came to the mountains to hunt, could the man who once used all this have been one of them?

His eyes strayed to the stuff sitting on the floor against the wall. A wooden bucket rested there filled with black walnuts and on top of them lay a powder horn. Apparently it had hung along with the haversack and canteen but had fallen from its place.

For the moment the haversack, canteen and powder horn were forgotten. Walnuts! How many had he cracked on the big rocks in and around Dogwood Flats? He grabbed up the bucket and hastily searched for a hammer, for he knew that in a tack-room a hammer was one of the essential tools that could always be found there.

In his native haunts he had never had to hunt for a tool to crack nuts. Two rocks were all that were necessary and rocks were every where, especially in Dogwood Flats. He grabbed the bucket of nuts and the hammer and an old axe blade and headed outside in a fast trot.

Bewilderment greeted him at the first glance of the sun. Why was it still in the east? It was supposed to be late afternoon. Something was terribly wrong. Was he still in the hay loft and dreaming? But no, the bucket of walnuts and the tools in his hands were real. At last he reached the only reasonable conclusion. He had slept through the night and well into the next morning!

Bill didn't want to remain in the open, so he headed for the thickly timbered knoll. He laid the tools in a heap and sat down where young pines had seeded around some larger trees. There concealed from the rest of the world on a thick carpet of pine needles he started cracking the walnuts. He knew he would have to be careful and not eat many at a time. He cracked the dry shells and pulled the big strodder jocks out and started munching.

He knew his empty stomach could very easily reject the rich flavorsome walnuts, so after just a few mouthfuls he laid his tool down and walked to the barn again. He felt strength already flowing through his being. He returned to the knoll with the haversack, canteen and powder horn. In case someone passed the barn he would be hidden with his treasures that would assure him at least a fighting chance at survival on his homeward journey.

Bill never stopped until he had cracked the last one of the walnuts. He put them in the haversack. By this time he was very thirsty but where the next drink would come from he had no idea.

He swung the bundles he had used for a pillow, the haversack and canteen over his back. He gathered up the tools and started his final trip back to the barn. He put the powder horn in the wooden bucket and when he laid the tools in their proper places he left the bucket where he found it after removing the powder horn. He carefully latched the tack-room door and walked down the long hall and took one final look at the comforting coziness of the building. It had served like a green oasis on a long desert journey but he knew as he closed the door and dropped the latch that he would never enter its welcoming walls again.

Thirst, like a haunting demon, tormented Bill's every step as the day wore one. He had decided to vary his northerly course to a more easterly direction in hopes of cutting across the stream he had found the day before.

After hours of strength sapping weariness he saw a thread of deeper yellowish green cutting through the landscape-willows! He thought, surely it must be willows.

Bill picked up his pace and soon the green thread widened into a broad band of ribbon. Before long he was standing in the water where willows gently swayed on the banks. He washed his hands and face. Then cupping his hands he drank mouthfuls of the life giving elixir.

Several days later found Bill climbing the foot-hills. He had gained in strength "due to the big mess of crayfish he had eaten". He had washed himself off again from head to toe, then he filled the canteen and was preparing to take leave of the little stream when he noticed the crayfish mounds thrown up on the banks. He opened the haversack and fished out the knife that lay in the bottom of the bag. He cut some limbs that grew along with the willows, which were stronger, and started digging.

Soon he had a big pile of crayfish. He would have eaten them raw but he had heard of people packing them in mud along river banks and baking them. He was afraid to raise a smoke here in this open country, so he did the next best thing. He took off his shirt and tied the crayfish up in its folds, then started following the stream. Late in the afternoon he found himself in a wooded area. Here in the dense timbers he felt it would be safe to start a fire.

That night was the first time he went to sleep with a full stomach since his capture. He untied his pack and put on the coat he had been carrying and lay down beside a fallen log in a pile of leaves. He spread the saddle blanket over his feet and fell asleep. He had moved on from the place where he had eaten his supper for fear a wild animal would catch the scent of the baked crayfish and attack him. As time passed reality and fancy seemed to merge at times. So much so that he would find himself startled at the sound of his own voice as he talked with an imaginary being but there was one memory clear and vivid, he would never forget and after that happening his mind became clear and he became his old self again. Fancy faded and the real world took shape again though harsh as it may have been and hope, like one of the wonderful plants that were pushing their way upward toward the sun, unfolded in his wounded heart.

While skirting wide from the main trail, he chanced upon a small clearing. It was only a little pocket tucked away in the skirt of a high and rugged mountain but something told him it was a friendly place.

The small cabin looked as if it had landed at random in the clearing from some place else and decided to stay. It stood near the eastern edge of the clearing where a babbling spring branch splashed and rippled on its rush down the steep mountain side between the cabin and the dark rim of the forest.

He stood in the deep shadows beneath the thick timber and looked longingly at the small snug building with its little wisp of smoke feathering out in the sweet smelling air.

A spring house squatted over the swift moving stream and some how he knew there would be a cow. He also knew she would not be in the clearing but hidden away somewhere in another field away from sight and that there would be no milk in the spring house for if soldiers should chance upon the place milk would be a dead give away and the cow would be slaughtered.

But where, he wondered would one keep milk if not in the spring house? Suddenly he knew the answer! Keeping low and moving stealthily he crept noiselessly through the thick wood fern and followed the branch up its rocky course until he found himself enclosed on both sides by a tangled mass of blackberry briars and willow sprouts, here the water course split a gash in the earth and steep banks loomed on either side.

A few yards up the bramble covered banks the water disappeared beneath the high northern embankment and he knew he had found the head of the spring.

At this juncture the space widened between the banks and as the water overflowed from the spring it spread out over the yellow sandy bottom. A gourd dipper with a hole through the neck hung from a broken twig and two earthen crocks were sunk half way in the chilling water. They were covered with wooden lids that were weighted down with stones from the branch and squatting before them with her feet planted on two flat rocks was a woman of undeterminable age.

He was sure he had made no sound and he stood motionless as the woman reached for the rock on top of the earthen crock but she sensed his presence and her arm stopped in mid air.

She turned her head and looked directly into his eyes. Suddenly the weakness that had plagued his every step that day prevailed and he sank down helplessly on a tuft cushion of mosses that grew beside the branch. The woman held the same position for several moments. Her hair, white as the dogwood blossoms, was parted in the middle and the thick wavy tresses were fastened in a loose bun at the back of her head.

Her hands were work worn and rough but her face wore a look of youth that belied her white hair and care worn hands but it was her eyes that commanded his attention. He had never seen eyes that color before. They were a yellowish brown that sparkled like polished stone, they were large and fringed with dark gold lashes and her brows were a shade between gold and a chestnut brown.

Suddenly she rose to her feet and reached for the gourd dipper. She rinsed it carefully in the spring water, then lifting the wooden lid from one of the crocks she dipped the gourd into the thick buttermilk which coated the outside of the gourd like a coat of white paint. She came and squatted before him and held the gourd to his lips. Neither had spoken during the whole interval. They were two souls that had met on the road of life and she understood his needs.

As he gulped down the cold liquid she pulled the gourd from his lips. Then she spoke for the first time in a voice as soft as the lapping water at her feet, "Take your time son, give the milk time to coat your stomach." Then raising her hand in a friendly gesture she whispered, "I'll be back." Bill sat there with the gourd of milk in his hands while his eyes followed his benefactor out of sight.

He slowly sipped the thick buttermilk while his eyes took in his surroundings in minute details. A bunch of dandelions bloomed in the edge of the branch, a big lizard wiggled his way up stream and he watched until it disappeared behind one of the rocks in the stream bed.

Crayfish mounds rose here and there near the head of the spring and his mind turned back to his home in Dogwood Flats. He thought of the many times he had dug out the family spring due to the pesky crayfish whose mound building changed the water course.

So lost was he in his thoughts the woman stood before him again without his being aware of her returning. She held out a small deep bowl which contained a piece of golden corn bread and a spoon. As he tried to thank her she placed her fingers on his lips and spoke to him in a tone usually reserved for a small child, "Go with God my boy and take this with you. You can call it your bag of hope."

She thrust a soft leather bag into his hands. Whoever had tanned the leather knew their business well, for the bag was soft and pliable, it was gathered at the top and tied with a narrow strip of the same soft leather and while he was lost in admiration and wonder at the bag and its contents, the woman slipped away.

He crumbled the corn bread and poured milk over it until the bowl was full. Then as the evening sun fell behind the mountains and the soft gloom of early evening settled around him he ate the first enjoyable meal since he had left the mountains. He washed the bowl and spoon in the branch and sat them down on one of the wooden crock covers. Then kneeling before the mossy cushion on which the leather bag lay he slowly untied the draw string that held the top together. He looked at the contents for several seconds then smiled in appreciation at the thoughtfulness of the kind lady who had befriended him for the bag was filled with big golden grains of parched corn. It was indeed a bag of hope, for it would give him strength to make his way over the steep mountains to his beloved valley where loved ones were waiting.

The Rebel Soldier

When Bill finally stepped through the gap in the mountain, it was a balmy day in early spring. The trees down below the gap that grew here and there in small clusters throughout the big steep field were not clearly defined. A dense sprouting of yellowish green leaves concealed their branches within their tender foliage blending the tree trunks with the other colors so the view that spread before him appeared unreal and more like a painting beneath the sun's warm glow.

On the far northeastern rim of Roan Mountain a patch of snow glittered belying the promise of continuing warmth. Bird song broke the silence as they flitted among the clumps of thicket carrying twigs to fashion into nests for their young.

Bill sank to the ground in a heap and his weary being gloried in the warm sunshine. He had been cold and hungry for so long. He closed his eyes there on the mountain side, too weary to drink in the beauty before him and he thought back over the long months since he had passed this way.

After resting in the sun for a while Bill opened his eyes and reached into his pocket and drew out the soft leather bag. It was his only proof that the whole episode had not been a figment of his imagination.

Carefully he folded the bag and stuffed it back into his pocket and the vision of a pair of eyes, deep and mysterious as bottomless pools swam through his memory and a face hauntingly beautiful, reflecting wisdom beyond the earthly realm of human understanding with all the pathos of the human family playing in shades of light and shadow over its delicate plane.

It was the face of woman kind, mother, sisters and sweetheart. All sharing the same bone structure, an everlasting face revealed in brief glimpses then lost forever on the winds of time.

Near the place where he sat a rock protruded from the earth with the resemblance of the head of a serpent. Ants worked in and out of the crack that formed its mouth and beside it a dried bunch of last year's milk weed with most of its pods intact despite the ravages of a harsh winter stood in molding dejection. He idly put forth his hand and squeezed one of the pods. Little glassy brown seeds attached to a downy substance as silky and pure as angel tresses floated on the gentle breezes that wafted across the face of Pumpkin Patch Mountain.

The milk weed brought to mind the prickly thistles that thrived in the old cow pastures of Dogwood Flats and how as a boy he had pulled their blooming top knots and chewed them to make "purple spit".

At the present he felt as weightless as the thistle-down and at the thought of himself rising to the heights of the tall timber and soaring beyond to float on the fleecy white clouds overhead threw him into a fit of hysterical laughter which shook his fragile frame like a trembling aspen in a wind storm, while tears of exhaustion stained his thin cheeks.

But unknown to him while he indulged in fancy and reflection in the sun on the face of the mountain a lone Confederate soldier who had been following him slipped through the gap and took the old Indian trail down the mountain for several hundred yards then turned west across the field and hid in a clump of bushes. In the meantime Bill decided to take the near-cut. He crossed the worm fence below the road and went down through the field for kin-folks lived in the house below.

A small ridge, like the back bone of a razor backed hog, humped up near the top of the big field. From that vantage point he could see clear down to the creek. He felt a shock charge through his being when he saw the fine old log house was missing. There was nothing but a pile of ashes, the smoke blackened chimney and a few scattered out buildings. As he stood there shaken by the sight, a dog horn sounded from the mountain above him. Bill knew nothing of the signals the settlers had worked out, so he continued his descent through the field and entered a small clump of bushes.

Suddenly the Confederate soldier stepped out from behind a tree. He had his gun pointed at Bill and his face wore a look of sneering contempt.

It was almost too much to bear for him. The unthinkable had happened, captured almost in sight of home. For a fleeting moment he toyed with the idea of refusing to move, to die there on the spot but the wicked looking gun barrel pointed at his stomach made him change his mind. The solider motioned with the gun barrel for him to start moving and Bill started slowly to retrace his steps up the path he had just descended.

Unknown to either Bill or the Confederate soldier, other eyes had witnessed the capture and followed every move as the two made their way up through the steep field. They reached the worm fence below the road and Bill crossed first. He went up the hill for a few yards until his captor ordered him to stop, then the soldier started to cross. He was astride the top rail and paused for a brief second before swinging over to the other side. That was his last conscious act. A gun belched flame from a thicket near by and the Rebel soldier pitched forward and fell on the opposite side of the rail fence, dead before he struck the ground from a bullet through the heart.[12]

The final chapter of Bill's brief and tragic life was soon to be written. As soon as he regained his health, he left his beloved valley to join the Union army but fate had not decreed for him to return alive.

After Bill left home long months passed before the family heard from him again. Then one day a messenger came with word that he was down with typhoid fever over in Limestone Cove, Tennessee. He and a McKinney man, his given name is not known, were on their way back from the war when they both were stricken with the dreaded disease.

---

[12] Down through the years since the Civil War the story of the Rebel soldier has often been told but neither Judy or Jane, who knew the intimate details of the happening, ever revealed the name of the person who fired the fatal shot or the identity of the Rebel soldier. They must have known his name for his every action pointed to the fact that he was familiar with the terrain. Perhaps he had been a childhood comrade of Bill's. Jane and Judy said he was buried up near the gap in the mountain close to the place where he met his death but no one knows today the exact location of his secret grave. In those awful days during the Civil War brother fought against brother and neighbor against neighbor, so people had to be close mouthed. If the identity of the Rebel soldier or the person who shot him was known to Bill's family, it was imperative it be kept a secret for fear of retaliation.

In the old days people believed that when a human life was taken a ghost always appeared to "hant" the place where the murder had been committed and the old folks told of a ghost that used to walk beside people as they carried their lanterns along the road that leads from the gap in the mountain down to Little Rock Creek bridge. They said all that could be seen of the ghost was its feet and part of its trouser legs and they could hear its footsteps on the gravel. Perhaps, as the old folks believed, it really was the ghost of the Rebel soldier who rose from his secret grave at night and it was his feet that marched beside people as he had once marched in the long ago days during the Civil War.

George Cook, Bill's father, hastened to their bedsides where he tended to their needs day and night. In the old days people killed many of their patients by their methods of doctoring. Fever victims were allowed no food except a little bread soaked in coffee, then the bread was strained from the coffee and a few spoonfuls were administered. They kept the sick person's lips moistened with a wet rag but no water was allowed to be swallowed.

George Cook, exhausted from the long vigil, sat dozing in his chair. Bill watched until his father's head slumped on his shoulder in a relaxed position and the sound of snoring penetrated the otherwise quiet room. Then he crept from beneath the covers and slipped noiselessly across the floor and drank long and deep from the dipper. Scarcely had he settled in bed again when his father awoke. George sensed something was amiss and with apprehension he looked at the water bucket where the dipper had been floating on the full bucket of water. Now it lay plunged to the bottom and he knew what had happened.

An old country doctor was summoned and when he arrived and was told the details he said in a somber tone, "the boy has just signed his death warrant". The doctor was right. Bill died a short time later.[13] He said if Bill had just taken a good drink little harm would have come from it but in his feverish thirst he had foundered on the water which meant certain death.

As cloth spinner of the thread of life clipped the last strand in the tapestry of Bill's young life, so closed another chapter in the history of the Cook family during the terrible days of the Civil War.

---

[13] Military records indicate that he died 27 February 1862 in Morristown, Tennessee. He is buried somewhere in Limestone Cove, Tennessee.

Sins Of Our Fathers

On a clear crisp day in mid-fall as the leaves lay on the ground like a thick brown carpet and the few dry ones that still clung to the branches of beech and oak trees trembled as the wind swept through the hollows and scattered the fallen ones like chicken feathers at molting time. A band of Union soldiers rode through the gap in the mountain and stopped briefly to view the terrain. The beauty of the countryside went unnoticed for they were men with souls as rough and callused from war as the scarred red face of Fork Mountain Bluff was scarred from the ravages of time. Instead their sharp eyes searched for the tell-tale signs of smoke that rose lazily from chimneys and hung in the air like a blue banner above the homesteads until the wind in its fury thrashed them to the ground as it passed in relentless flight across the barren hills.

One of the men in the group was a colored man and to quote a phrase, he was "as tall as a Georgia pine", without an ounce of excess fat on his giant frame. As he slipped from the saddle he began to sing an old Negro spiritual, "Well, I looked over Jordan and what did I see, coming forth to carry me home? A band of angels coming after me, coming forth to carry me home."

From high up on the mountain to the west of the gap a dog horn sounded three blasts, a pause, then three more in rapid succession, the signal of approaching danger. From another high ridge farther up the mountain toward Dogwood Flats the signals were answered.

The Union soldiers seeing smoke curling up from the nearest house, which happened to be the one where old Granny Cook had once lived and now had passed on to another generation, headed in that direction. Soldiers acting as scouts went on foot down through the field, while the commanding officer along with several other soldiers took the horses around the road. Dismounting in the yard they surrounded the house, banging loudly on the doors, demanding entrance, then when only a few seconds had passed, using their shoulders against the heavy wooden doors, they crashed their way into the house. An elderly woman, bent and frail, stood near the kitchen door. In her arms she held a small child that whimpered with fright as the soldiers entered. The old woman spoke in a voice that belied her weak appearance, "If'n you had aheld on I was afixen to open the door. Hit's a might hard to hold a young'un and work the door handle at the same time." "Well, you shore took your own easy time", one of the soldiers said rudely. Neither the white haired old lady or the child aroused any feelings of pity on his part. He was saddle sore and hungry and by the looks of the place he doubted if there was enough food in the house to fill one stomach, let alone a whole band of soldiers.

Climbing the ladder that led to the loft, the soldier fumbled around in the darkness until he found the window shutter. As light streamed in he found nothing but two old shuck mattresses and a few sheep skins. Descending from the loft he and two other soldiers searched every hole and cranny but not a bite of food did they find. The other soldiers searched the outbuildings with the same results. The soldiers began to question the old woman who sat in a rocking chair. The child closed its eyes and wept silently as she cradled it in her bony arms. "What you people live on here? Nobody can live on the wind, although you look mighty like you do. Where is the food you got stashed away?"

The old woman calmly rocked back and forth, as she answered their question with a question. "What would you eat ifen soldiers took everything you worked for? Ifen raiders rode in at night and took your kiver and vitals? I'll tell you what! I got out the other day and dug wild artichokes to keep from starving to death. I buried them in the yard, go dig them up and help yourself to them fer there wuz two left."

Even the hardened soldiers felt subdued as she lashed out at them with withering scorn. Just then the big colored man blocked the doorway and for the first time the old woman felt a shiver of fear, for some unknown reason she had always been afraid of colored people and when she looked into the dark depths of his eyes her gaze was not as steady as it had been when she had mocked the soldiers.

"Come on out", the colored man called from the doorway. "I've got me a notion there's food around these parts." He paced up and down for a few moments as if deep in thought. When all the soldiers had gathered around he said, "Ifen I had some'fen to hide I know I wouldn't hide it in the out buildings or in the house. So I'm agoin to take me a look-see down along the creek bank."

He started off at a fast trot then called over his shoulder, "I'ze also knows there's mor'n the old woman and young'un who lives in dat house. I could swear it on old John Brown's grave!" At the colored man's words the soldiers started looking with renewed vigor but found nothing. After an interval of perhaps twenty minutes they gave up altogether.

Suddenly, at the sound of a loud whistle, they looked toward the creek where the colored man, grinning from ear to ear, came up the bank leading a cow. "I found her in a kind of walled up cellar down by the creek. It was covered with willow sprouts and looked like a brush heap!"

Inside one of the outbuildings behind a false wall that had been constructed soon after soldiers had first appeared on Little Rock Creek, the rest of the family crouched in cramped positions. Through a tiny crack in the wall the man of the house peered out as the colored man led the cow into the yard and at that moment every mean and hurtful thing concerning the war was the color of black and all the hatred it had spawned was focused on the black man. The man heard the outside door squeak and the thumping of booted feet inside the building. They all held their breathe until the door squeaked shut again.

On the outside of the false wall a sheep skin concealed the door that was just barely large enough for a man to crawl through. Old pieces of harness and raw hide throngs, along with many different kinds of dried herbs and barks, camouflaged the wall of the hiding place. On the adjoining walls a roll of sheep skins swung loosely from a wooden peg and a tanned piece of raw hide was also stretched on the wall so the sheep skin covering the secret door wouldn't look too conspicuous. Two large wooden barrels set in each corner against the false wall and split baskets hung there and completed the interior setting.

After what seemed like hours to the people scrounged into the almost airless space, the soldiers began preparing to take their leave. They had slaughtered the cow in the yard and the smell of the roasting meat had made them more aware of their loss, for the milk and butter had been their main source of food and the cow had been born and raised on the farm and had been a prized family possession.

Suddenly from the top of the high ridge the dog horn signaled again. This time one long blast, a pause, then another blast, and another. It was the signal of approaching Confederate soldiers.

Suddenly shooting broke loose outside. Apparently the Confederate soldiers had rode up Little Rock Creek instead of entering the valley through the gap. The man in the cramped hiding place whispered to the rest of the family to stay where they were and keep quiet. He was boiling mad because the colored man had found his cow and he intended to make the soldiers pay in any way he could. His trusty gun hung on the wall above his head and he felt along the rough logs until his groping fingers touched the cold metal of the gun barrel. Quickly he unfastened the door and crawled out through the small opening.

By now gun fire was sounding all along the creek bank and he knew his life was in jeopardy but this anger carried him beyond the brink of reason. Scarcely had he cleared the secret door and closed it again, when he heard a noise outside. Suddenly the door swung groaningly on its leather hinges. It was wood scraping on wood that made the almost human sounds. In the gloom of the building the man had the advantage as the big colored man stepped through the door he was felled like a giant tree by a single blow on the head.

Working fast the man tied him securely with the raw hide throngs that hung handy on the wall and gagged him with his own handkerchief. He felt along the floor that was cluttered with straw and shucks and lifted up a section that covered a root cellar. It took all the man's strength to drag the big colored man to the edge and roll him over into the gaping hole. He whispered fiercely as he lowered the covering, "You ist dug yourn own grave!" Carefully raking back the straw and clutter over the floor, the man started for the door when he heard loud voices in the yard. Scurrying like a frightened animal he squeezed through the secret door just in the nick of time, "Ain't no stink'in blue bellies in heah!", a deep voice yelled out. "Guess they're all together up along the creek bank."

The man glued his eyes to the small crack in the wall and felt his stomach muscles tighten with fear as he saw his mother, carrying his small son emerge from the house, two Confederate soldiers walking behind her. Once in the yard one of the soldiers grabbed her and shook her until her hair slipped loose from the twist she fashioned on top of her head. It swayed in the wind like a veil of white mist around her fragile shoulders. The terrified child began to wail in a wheezing kind of voice which made the soldier more furious than he already was, "Make that brat shut up before I throw him in the creek!" The thin high pitched voice was cut off in mid air just as if a hand had clamped around its windpipe. The child understood only too well and terror cut off his wind and silenced his vocal cords.

But the old woman's eyes blasted furiously, "You're a brave one. You air apickin on old women and young'uns. Askin me why I fed Union soldiers, when they killed my only cow right here in the yard. Ifen you want to see the blood ist look!" The Confederate soldier eyed her scornfully and said in a sarcastic tone, "You had a big helping of meat on your plate when we caught you red handed. That don't look like you wuz too heart broken over the old cow. I know you gave that cow to them Yankee soldiers, then set stuffing yourself on the left overs. Deny that old woman ifen you can!" "I don't deny feeding the child and myself, after all, it was my cow and they kilt her. Why shouldn't I eat my own meat after one uv them soldiers brung me a plateful? At least he had a heart and that's mor'n I can say fer you."

At her words the soldier rushed to the porch. From a pile of pine-knots that were used for torches, he selected a big rosiny one and ran to the bed of live coals where the Union soldiers had roasted the beef. He held it in the embers until it burst into bright flames that eat hungrily at the rosin, then he raced back past the old woman and child and vanished inside the house. Moments later he came out again laughing like a hyena. "You won't feed any more blue bellies in that house.", he told her with an evil grin on his cruel face.

As smoke rose in angry billows from the building the two Confederate soldiers leading their mounts slipped stealthily along the creek bank trying to get behind their enemies and hoping to surprise them while their attention was focused on the opposite side of the creek but the smoke from the burning building attracted the attention of one of the Union soldiers. As he looked toward the fire he saw the two Confederate soldiers creeping along through the trees and opened up fire. His first bullet felled one of the Rebels and a blast from an unknown location felled the other one. The two Rebel's horses frightened at the gun fire headed up the creek bank and vanished from view. The Rebel soldiers now badly out numbered, decided they had had enough. As they fled up Little Rock Creek the Union soldiers followed in hot pursuit. Gun fire echoed for perhaps a mile and a half then the Rebel soldiers threw down their guns and surrendered.

The Rebel soldiers were forced to bury their dead, then marched before their captors along the road. The Union soldiers gathered back at the place where the skirmish had started, where they attended the wounded but not a trace of the big colored man could they find. It was as if he had vanished from the face of the earth.

Meanwhile the family hidden behind the secret wall had found the heat unbearable. Amid the smoke and excitement, they managed to escape to a laurel patch along the creek bank below the ford but the old woman and child remained by the smoking rubble that had been their home.

When the Union soldiers took their leave, along with their Confederate prisoners and the all-clear signal sounded and re-echoed from the hills, people began to gather to offer what comfort they could. The loss the family had suffered was too deep for tears. It was friends and neighbors who wept as the dying rays of the sun turned the tops of the mountains a fiery red.

As the family stood huddled together staring into the live embers and women wiped the tears from their eyes on their apron tails, the few men present stood uneasily about, unable to release their emotions through tears. Their frustrations gave vent through verbal abuse of the brutes who had done this terrible thing. One old timer, who walked in a strutting manner due to a stiff knee, shook his fists in helpless fury and swore he would like nothing more than to roast the Rebel pigs in the glowing embers then like a shot the man whose home lay in smoking ruins leapt into the air, the expression on his face was like a wild man's.

"Wait!", he yelled. "I know where somebody is that is better'n all them stink'in Rebels put together, he's the big black nigger who found Maw's cow down by the creek!"

If a cannon ball had exploded in the field its effect would not have been more startling. "A nigger?" the words re-sounded among the group. "Come on, I'll show you", the man shouted, as he ran toward the outbuilding that had miraculously escaped the fire, with the group of people following.

Suddenly a puff of wind swept up the creek, driving smoke and ashes in their faces. The man groped for the door, then doubled over in a spasm of coughing. "Some body light a torch." Some one in the crowd yelled and the old man with the stiff knee headed for the building where old Granny Cook had first set up housekeeping. He had seen the interior of the old building in broad daylight and knew where to search. He grabbed a pine knot and stopped long enough to bury it in the smoldering fire, then holding the long torch high so the people could see their way, then lowering the flame so as not to set the building on fire he entered and held the light so the men could lift the floor planks that covered the root cellar.

It was a night no one in the little group would ever forget. In the torch's flickering glow that made the shadows play grotesquely on the walls and over the colored man's face whose large dark eyes, widened by fear, seemed to engulf them with their hypnotic stare and the women shrank back instinctively at his least movement, although his legs and hands were bound securely.

Outside by the flickering light of the torch the old woman faced the colored man once more, though the circumstances were reversed, her fear gave way to bitterness as she spoke accusingly, "You kilt old Daisy, you did. I had her hid down by the creek and I tended to her eve'r day, but you went asnooping around like a hound dog hunt'un fer eggs. I raised her from a calf of three days old ater her Maw was kilt by some kind of varmint up in the mountain pasture." The old woman turned her head and looked at the sleeping child who was held by its mother, "and my grand young'un there, I don't know how hit will make hit now with no milk, hit takes a hog of a person to do a thing like that ist to fill his stomach."

"Well," the old man with the stiff knee remarked, "hogs air fer roast'in and we already have the embers from this poor old woman's house that was burned down through low down meanness." The colored man's voice shook as he said in almost a whisper, "it wuz the Rebels who sot fire to her house, not me." "But you wuz the one who acted the hog. No telling what you'd a done if'n the Rebels hadn't showed up", the old man said accusingly.

"We wuz afixin to leave when the Rebels rode up and started shootin. Our stomachs were full and we meant no body no harm. Hit's the stinkin Rebs that burns and destroys." "You know fellers", one of the men spoke up, "this old hog here is too poor to roast ist now, though it's a shame to waste these embers. Let's fatten him up first!" What you mean, Jake?" one of the men asked. "Well, you know them logs we snaked down off'n the mountain and is piled up below the gap? Let's build a pen and fatten this here hog afore we kill him!" "Sounds mighty good to me", another voice chimed in, "Somebody git the torches and don't forget the axe and we'll get this old hog settled fer the night!"

For the next several days beautiful weather prevailed, as the season wore its beguiling veil of promise winter seemed far away. The deceptive air of peace made hope spring anew in the hearts of many but one destitute soul languished amid the lull between autumn's warmth and winter's icy cold. The colored man moaned and prayed in his cramped quarters. He begged for mercy but his pleas fell on deaf ears.

Children sometimes brought his food and they gawked at him through the cracks between the logs as if he was some sort of animal instead of a man. They seemed astonished at his ability to talk as they stood on the outside of the pen and sometimes tried to punch him with sharp sticks. A few times the frail old lady whose cow he had slaughtered carried his food up through the field in a slop bucket. His diet consisted of dish water, apple and potato peelings. Bread crumbs were precious commodities to be hoarded for the family's use and seldom had a crumb been dropped into the bucket of slop which was poured through an outside spout that emptied into a trough.

The man implored the old lady each time she appeared at the pen to help him escape. One time as she looked down through the cracks in the logs a ray of sunlight struck the colored man's face and seemed to lodge in his eyes. They were dark as a bottomless pool in the shadow but in the sunlight their color was as brown as a new buckeye that had just dropped to the ground. The old woman pondered on their changeable color and the haunting quality that lurked in their depths and her heart, despite herself, went out to him in that moment.

Then she spoke to him in a voice so low he could barely hear her words, "You ist tell me how somebody with my frame can lift off the top of this here pen, then I'll under take hit. Bad as I hate you for what you did to old Daisy, I don't want the blood of the likes of you on my hands when I go to the grave."

The old woman tried to talk to the men on the colored man's behalf but to no avail. When they brought his next meal they leaned against the pen and discussed the weather. They said he would be fat enough to kill as soon as the weather turned cold enough to salt him down. As the man sobbed and pled for his life inside the log structure a passer-by who had come through the gap left the wagon road and walked down and joined the men at the pen, he commented in a mocking tone, "You know it sounds almost as ifen that old hog is atalking. Come to think uv hit, I've heard niggers who couldn't talk much plainer." The men guffawed and slapped their legs and the colored man tried to close his mind against their cruelty.

As the men walked away from the pen the wailing of the wind blended with the wails of human misery over the ridges of a pitiless land. The weather changed during the night. Clouds scurried across the mountains from the north like rushing waves on a dark ocean and soon the face of Fork Mountain Bluff was obscured from view and crusty ice, thin as a knife blade, rimmed the edges of Little Rock Creek.

The wind, cold and cruel as the hearts of the men who held the Negro prisoner, whined as it thrust its relentless strength against the field where the log pen perched precariously on its steep slope. Within its cruel confines the Negro man, half frozen to death, knew he had spent the last day of his earthly pilgrimage when he looked out between the logs and saw a group of men approaching and heard the crunch of footsteps on the spewed up ground. One of the men carried a double bladed axe over his shoulder.

The man's throat closed so tight no sound escaped his still lips as the pen was slowly uncovered and rough hands reached for him. He offered no resistance as he was dragged to his feet. Fingers locked in his thick curly hair and pulled, until his neck lay stretched across the top log of the pen. The man with the axe braced his feet firmly, then swung the wicked looking axe high. With a single blow the head was severed from the man's body which slipped down to the floor of the pen, where the hands moved in feeble motions in the thick blood that spurted all over the logs and soaked the victims clothing. The head was thrown on top of the body while the lips still moved and the eyes, wide and staring, seemed to be looking into the depths of each man's soul.

At that moment the first snow flakes of the season began to fall. They were large and fluffy, like feathers from a huge pre-historic bird. There was a stillness in the air that made time stand still. It did not take long for the snow to begin to accumulate as the people began to seek shelter. Soon the marks of violence in the land was covered. The huge pike of ashes that had once been home to so many people throughout the long years since it had existed lay inches below the covering of white. It was as if mother nature, in a moment of gentleness, had decided to hide all the ugliness beneath her cleansing blanket from the eyes of the people who had already seen so much.[14]

---

[14] The story of the be-heading of the colored man has been handed down through the Cook family from generation to generation and I can well remember the goose pimples that crawled up and down my back each time I heard my father retell the grizzly tale.

The Jane Bald

After the Civil War the world that had once existed, lay in shambles. The people on Little Rock Creek struggled desperately just to merely exist. Most of the well built houses and barns lay in ashes due to the raiders, soldiers and corrupt home guard who had contributed to the destruction for their own selfish gain.

Crops had to be planted and there was no time to hew logs for new buildings. Even with time, man power was short. Several had died in the war, others were crippled or too broken spiritually to try again.

Discouragement flaunted its ugly colors and for many only the necessity of survival moved them to make a new start. Hastily built pole cabins with dirt floors such as the early settlers had built dotted the countryside. The people in Dogwood Flats were as poor as church mice. Large families crowded into one room cabins. Often housekeeping was set up with nothing more than a fireplace and one or two iron pots. Some families who had no bedding what so ever rolled up in sheep skins before the open fireplace.

But as the seasons changed, so did the hearts of the people. Hope, like a small flame on a winter day that is fed twigs until the whole fireplace is ablaze with warmth, began to flare once again and some of the residents in Dogwood Flats found employment over in Ripshin, Tennessee.[15]

On a crisp day in mid November Judy stood with her little two year old nephew's hand clasped tightly in her own which was small and care worn and watched as the winding path and dense timber swallowed her two sisters from view. Try as she would, she could not quell the feeling of apprehension as she gazed up the steep mountainside long after they had disappeared from sight.

According to the old timers, a headless ghost has haunted the gap since the days of the Civil War. It staggers around with groping hands and out stretched arms and in late fall, when the moon is full and the keening wind whispers as it sucks up Little Rock Creek, a moaning sound is carried on its chilling breath, as if the pathos of all the whole colored race were voiced in unison. It is a sound they declare, "like the cry of slavery", that once heard will never be forgotten.

[15] I have heard the old folks speak many times of an old Civil War veteran whom they referred to as Capt'n Nelson. One of Captain Nelson's legs had been almost blown off. They patched him up and saved his leg but he suffered from that old war wound for the rest of his life. Since he was handicapped he needed help to work his land and he was able to pay them for to put it in the old timer's words, "he drawed a war pension."

New acquaintances sprung up between the people of Dogwood Flats and the residents of Ripshin. Two of George Cook's daughters married and settled there. One's name was Lannie and the other Madeline. Two of George's grandsons also settled in Tennessee. Their names were George and Johnny. Johnny's daughter, Sallie (Mrs. Walter Church) settled in Unicoi. One of Johnny's children was named William (curly headed Will) due to William being a much used family name.

Johnny, George, Ruben, Lemuel and Fayette Cook were Mary Cook's children. Steven Cook also had a son name William (Little Will). He was foreman in the Cranberry mines for many years after leaving Little Rock Creek. He made his home in Avery County. Jim Cook had a son named William. This Will Cook ran a taxi service from Bakersville for several years and is still remembered as taxi driving Will.

On the other hand Jane and her younger sister Harriet faced the prospect of crossing over Roan Mountain to visit relatives in Ripshin, Tennessee as a pleasurable adventure. The terrible fear and anxiety they had lived through during the Civil War now lay behind them. Although many of the scars that had seared their very being had healed, others lay raw and sore and flared up at unexpected times for their spiritual wounds were deep and slow in healing and they had suffered casualties as surely as the wounded soldiers on the bloody battle field, even though their pains were not constant. Memories flashed as sharp as a knife blade cutting at their heart strings. Terrible memories too strong to die.

It was in the late spring and early summer when Jane felt the loss of her beloved brother Bill more intensely. Even the flowers that bloomed so brightly in her father's yard were reminders of things better forgotten. The haunting image of his young troubled face hung in the web of her memory as stubborn as the strands of the spider web that clings to its hapless victim but on that particular day two sisters were determined to put the past behind them. Life had to be lived and the few joys that came during its short span had to be gathered and enjoyed like the flowers by the wayside whose blooming seasons were brief.

After assuring Judy they would be in no danger for the leaves were down and they could see their way, so there was no danger of their taking the wrong trail and getting lost. They gaily climbed the mountain leaving Dogwood Flats and their daily cares behind.

The mountain beckoned with their charms of cold springs and many lofty resting places and the wind sang in the bare tree tops as they wound their way along ancient paths first trampled by the feet of Indian braves and wild animals.

Suddenly a scream, much like the voice of a woman, split the silence as they threaded their way through the thick balsams on the slopes of Roan Mountain and they hastened their pace to almost a trot until they reached the meadow that stretched for miles along the open face of the mountain.

There on the balds where only rhododendron and other small shrubs grew, they could see in all directions and they felt much safer for they knew the scream they had heard had not been a human cry but the scream of a panther and they were glad they could reach Ripshin before the shadows of evening closed about them.

Meanwhile back in Dogwood Flats Judy continued to fret and worry. She had a premonition something awful was about to happen to her two sisters and no amount of persuasion from the other members of the family could convince her otherwise.

On the morning Jane and Harriet left Ripshin on their return trip the air was much cooler than when they had arrived but the sky was blue with only a few thin gossamer like clouds appearing, then feathering out into nothingness as they sailed southward. Jane observed their fleeting course and knew cooler weather was on its way, then for the first time she noticed how pale her sister Harriet's face looked in the mid-morning light and as the day progressed they walked at a much slower pace for Harriet became tired and weak.

Jane was plagued with gnawing pangs of remorse for not heeding Judy's pleas to them to wait a few more days before starting on their hard journey over the mountains to Ripshin. Judy's argument had been that Harriet had not sufficiently recovered from a bout of the dreaded milk sickness to undertake such a long walk up and down the steep mountain slopes but Harriet appeared to have fully recovered so they had brushed aside all doubts concerning Judy's fears.[16]

Now Jane was sure her sister was suffering from a reoccurrence of the disease and she was terribly frightened for they still had the steepest part of the mountain to climb and her sister was barely able to keep on her feet. Soon Harriet was wracked with nausea and trembled like the dry leaves that still clung to the beech trees as the harsh winds tried to dislodge them.

The day wore on like an endless nightmare. The wind that had driven the clouds high in the sky in early morning now whipped low through the deep hollows and howled like a hungry wolf on the mountain top, as Jane clung to her sister, urging her to take another step up the steep grade.

Finally, as twilight settled in the deep hollows they reached the summit where after a few tortured steps Harriet collapsed beneath a pine tree in the edge of the bald. Jane knew by her sister's condition this was as far as she would ever be able to go, so she made her as comfortable as possible amid the mounds of moss and dry pine needles and wept bitterly at their plight as night fell like a dark curtain over the earth.

There on the mountain with the wind crying like a living thing, its gusts as cold and sharp as the grim reapers' scythe with wild animals sounding their mournful cries from the ridges below and the weak voice of her sister begging for help, time became an undeterminable force. It could have been only a few hours but it seemed to Jane like a thousand midnights all rolled up into one but sometime along that lonely passage of black misery Harriet ceased to utter a sound. Jane held her close and tried to keep her warm but the night turned bitterly cold and the ground froze and spewed up around them. Jane had no light or any means of starting a fire. There was no chance of her finding her way through the blackness to get help. There was nothing to do but listen to the wind as it shrieked and raged and mocked at her helplessness.

Finally the heavens began to lighten and a rosy glow like the flush on a cherub's face spread across the wide expanse above her head and Jane rose to her almost frozen feet and began to make her way downward through the misty chill of pre-dawn. Down below the summit the fog hung in thick ghostly shrouds with the balsam boughs sticking through the milky whiteness like dark groping arms.

Finally she reached a homestead in Roan Valley, which at that time was sparsely settled, and when the man of the house heard of her plight he hurriedly hitched up a team and wagon, then loaded on some bedding. By the time Harriet's unconscious and half frozen form was lifted and place amid the thick covers in the wagon bed the red sun, like a ball of fire, shone through the morning mists casting an eerie glow across the grassy bald and Jane pulled the covers over her sister's face to close out the chilling damp air and to hide the death pallor that shone so plainly on her drawn features.

When her sisters failed to show up Judy distraught and tearful wrung her hands and paced the floor, refusing to be comforted. She begged the men folks to go look for her sisters but they pointed out how futile it would be to look for them before daylight. They told her Jane and Harriet had just decided to spend one more night in Ripshin and that they would be back

[16] Milk sickness is caused by the cow eating loco weed and then transmitting the illness to humans. Milk from an infected cow makes the drinker violently ill and a high fever follows the infection. Antidotes for it are few, though the use of white snakeroot has been recommended.

safe and sound, although the men had begun to feel anxious themselves for Jane knew the weather signs and they could not understand why she would linger on the other side of Roan Mountain with a possible blizzard threatening to snow them in.

Judy urged the men to leave early the next morning but they reasoned it would be more sensible to wait a few hours and give them time to reach home before starting the search. There were many different trails leading across the mountains. Who knew which trail they would choose?

At last due to Judy's frantic urging the men started out on their journey northward toward Ripshin but they had barely reached the wagon road that led up through Dogwood Flats when a wagon and team came into view around the sharp bend where the road led out from the steep creek bank at the southern end of the community.

As the team and wagon approached they recognized the driver and when they heard the tragic news they knew Judy's fears had been well founded. Harriet died shortly after reaching Dogwood Flats. It was November 17, 1870. As Jane stood alone on the Fork Mountain graveyard long after everyone else had left, she listened as her Grandmother Isabel had listened on that fateful day so long ago to the herald of another storm, this one a winter blizzard. Above her head the tree tops trembled in fear as the wind muttered veiled warnings that were destined to become an open conflict between them. They, with their roots sunk deep beneath the surface of the earth, with grown rings proving they had spent more time on earth than any living mortal, seemed to have the advantage but who could stand and face such a formidable force, who with one giant stroke could uproot the most powerful among them? Therefore, they bowed in servile surrender before their invisible master who lashed them cruelly in his relentless rage. Even the mourning doves had fled from the hills and Jane watched the first snow flakes of the coming blizzard fall like white downy feathers only to disappear into nothingness when they fell on the raw earth that now housed her sister's body.

Her wish was that she, like the doves, could escape to a land of forgetfulness. Guilt, like the grave worms that would eventually destroy her sister's body gnawed at her conscience but time would not turn back and so closed another chapter in the history of her family.

Many years in the future from that November day in 1870 when the last page of her earthly pilgrimage had been written Jane needed no epitaph chiseled in stone to preserve her memory, like a slumbering yellow spider above the weby mists of Roan Valley The Jane Bald stands a perpetual monument in her honor, a lasting memorial that will every exist throughout all enduring time.

Figure 1 Harriet Cook with dog, Polly Cook standing, Jane Cook sitting.

Flight of the Ravens

When his many family members were gathered together on some special occasion George Cook often observed their individual habits and as the stars differ in their brightness, so were his children diverse one from another in looks and personalities.

Among his many daughters, Judy, though small and fragile as a Dristan China doll was the one endued with the most inner strength. It was an endowment that drew people to her "as a moth is drawn to a flame". She possessed a spiritual glow that cast its brightness to all around her despite the manner in which she dressed, which consisted of solid black garments.

And of all his sons, Sylvester "Sill" was the one who cast his light at a different angle. His inquiring mind and thirst for knowledge coupled with the fact that he was also a dreamer set him apart from his brothers. Most of George's other sons loved to till the good earth because they enjoyed the things it brought forth. It left little more to be desired.

But to Sill it was the means of his daily bread but little more. He loved the smell of the ground while digging and hoeing. His brothers saw only the green stalks of corn, the promise of bread for their table and feed for their cattle but the fragrance of the sassafras roots which ran below the surface of the earth in the rich new grounds filled Sill's heart with more pleasure than the stalks of corn ever could.

The family would hoe a round of corn, then rest beneath a shady tree. As the others discussed the crops and things in general Sill held his peace and dreamed. He longed to have more books to read but times were hard, for the mountain settlers had never fully recovered from the devastating effects of the Civil War and extra items were hard to come by. Sometimes he would walk for miles to borrow a book. Oft times, lost within its pages, time slipped by unnoticed and only the fading light served as a reminder of its passage.

Sometimes when he slipped away to be by himself to read, he followed an old cow trail and ended up in a private place amid a laurel thicket. There in a world all his own he read without interference. At other times, "depending on his mood", he followed the branch, walking on moss covered rocks that stuck up along and amidst its meandering course until he found a hidden nook that suited his fancy.

He had learned to read at an early age, "due to Judy's tutoring", and was now a magistrate. The only other person who had entered his private world was Nora, the girl he intended to marry. Sill had a book of old British Ballads, old and worn when he received it as a gift. The meaning of many of the hard to pronounce words he grasped only in a vague sense but he loved them never the less and in his mind he often tried to fathom what the ancient far away world of his ancestors had been like. Through the different writings he caught glimpses of green rolling hills, of blue waters, of wild moors, of battles, of peaceful country side and shady lanes and through the whole fabric ran a golden thread of romance with tragedy winding its own black strand in tangled fashion throughout the pattern.

Those he often read to Nora as they sat in some hidden glen or recited them as they walked together, hand in hand, along the laurel choked paths that criss-crossed the western section of Dogwood Flats, for he had read them so often he knew most of them by heart. Even if some of their meanings were obscure, the pathos in their haunting language struck a responding cord deep within both of the young peoples' hearts.

Sill and Nora made a handsome couple. He with his tall slender frame and fair complexion, his best features being his smoky blue gray eyes with tiny golden flecks which reminded Nora of water lilies floating on blue-green water and his hair which tumbled over his forehead in thick heavy waves, in color, a light glossy brown, made her think of the wind waves in a wheat field at harvest time.

Nora was small but well rounded with a complexion as soft as the petals of the wild roses that bloomed in tangled masses among the split rail fences that wormed their way across the hill sides and her hair, the color of yellow sun touched clouds on a crisp winter day, hung below her waist line when loose in thick ropy coils.

But as the spring is brief in its budding awakening, so was their time of dreaming brief, as a rose bud chilled by a late spring cold-snap, their plans like the rose petals were never to unfold, nipped in the bud by the chilling hand of the grim reaper.

The summer fled, or so it seemed to the young couple, like the fleeting clouds that sailed over Roan Mountain when driven by the north wind. Soon the sound of frost Jacks and other fall insects serenaded them as they walked through the crisp fall air from the corn shucking that courting couples enjoyed so much. There were games played. Sometimes between the courting couples and sometimes between the boys and the girls. If the boys won they got to kiss the girls of their choice and vice versa. The old people laughed and relived their own memories as they heard the giggles from the young girls whose blushes were hidden by the shadows of the dimly lit crib sheds.

Soon bed ticks were stuffed until they almost burst at the seams with shredded shucks and old cows chewed in contentment while the rest of the shucks lasted. Before the last crib shed was emptied and the long golden ears of corn were piled in the corn cribs the night air had turned from being crisp to down right cold. Frost glittered in the moonlight and the cold ground crunched beneath their feet. But Sill and Nora didn't mind, their numbed feet soon thawed when they crawled into the over stuffed shuck beds that were already heated from the body warmth of brothers and sisters. The young couple walked beneath the dark expanse of a cloudless sky and gazed at the twinkling stars that glittered like chunks of gold. In mountain folk-lore they had been told that stars were really not stars at all, but holes in the sky where the golden streets of heaven shone through and to them during that season, it was not hard to believe. It was an enchanting time when anything seemed possible.

As Sill looked at the beauty of the night as the moon rode high and proud through the heavens, he wondered if sometime in the far away future if the whole covering of the sky would not be rolled back to reveal now invisible world far above the clouds. "Well", he mused out loud, as he viewed the starry expanse, "Ifen there's no stars up there, that old sky is agetting mighty raggedy!" Nora added her thoughts after considering the mountain folk-lore. "Anything with that many holes is liable to fall apart at any moment. Imagine no more shinny dots of gold across the sky and no moon! Nothing but a solid gold sky which is heaven's floor."

At that moment a cold gust of wind swept through the old cow pasture and Nora pulled at Sill's hand, "Come on! Let's get out uv this cold night air before we both catch our death uv cold." Little did she realize how prophetic her words were to be. Sill had had a cold for the past several days but his condition had not worsened so he had ignored his scrappy throat and short breath. Nora, on the other hand was well aware of the curse of weak lungs[17] that plagued the Cook family and had voiced her fears about his setting in the cold crib shucking

---

[17] Records have shown that several died of consumption or tuberculosis.

corn especially after the weather turned cold but he only laughed her worries away and insisted on helping shuck the last crib of corn.

At the beginning of the corn shucking season Nora had felt a sense of foreboding as she had listened to the dire predictions of the old folks. "Ravens", they said, "were a bad omen", as they lifted their wrinkled faces toward the heavens and watched three of the inky black creatures cross the sky on their westward course. Later when one of the old timers, whose eyes were too weak and watery to scan the blue circle of sky, was told of the flight of the ravens, she had asked their number and when she was told she said sagely, "It's a warning, sometimes a terrible storm follows their flight this time of year but three ravens flying west means a death." She had brushed the old lady's warning aside, after all, the old folks had a saying for everything and she was young and the hand of death seemed far away.

That night was to be the last time they would ever walk beneath the ragged dome of a starry heaven. They would never again ramble along the old cow trails that twisted across the hillsides and through the deep hollows like the path of a serpent. Instead the next path Nora would follow with him was to be the old dug road, so named because the path had been too narrow for men to carry a coffin up the steep winding trail to the cemetery at the summit of the hill. Therefore the men of Dogwood Flats took their mattocks and shovels and dug out the laurel roots and widened the road so a team and sled could easily traverse its steep course.

The cold Sill had neglected turned into the dreaded fever and the efforts loved ones made to try and save his life only worsened his condition. The bright light of his young life that had glowed with such promise was snuffed out while Nora stood helplessly by. Once more the earth was opened at the top of the laurel hill and the fresh red clay colored the brown grave side and left red splotches after the grave was filled in which reminded Nora of the blood of some strange sacrifice, as if the earth, ever hungry, had demanded a young vital victim to assuage its endless cravings. [18]

---

[18] At the time of his death Sylvester "Sill" Cook lived with his sister Sarah (Sally) in a one room house on what is now known as the Riley Cook property in the lower section of Dogwood Flats. The property has changed hands several times since Sill died. It was once owned by Jesse and Hattie Cook. They added a kitchen to the house. The place was once owned by Thomas Burleson. Riley and Laura Cook was the last to buy the property and one of the sons owns it at the present time.

Riley and his family lived in the old Sallie house, as it was known, until they built a new one sometime in the nineteen and thirties. Then the old house was torn down. The cold free running spring near the western property line once supplied most of the families in the lower section of Dogwood Flats with their drinking water. Although there were other springs in the valley and other families had plenty of wash water from the two branches that still flows through the lower section, the water from that particular spring was preferred, even if it had to be carried from a longer distance, because of its clearness and purity. It never settled and left a mud film in the water bucket as most of the other springs did.

Eventually Nora married another man. She told some of the women in the Cook family she only married her husband because his face in profile reminded her of her lost love.

The description of Sill was given to me by the present John Hopson. He told me he had heard his parents describe Sill many times. John's father, David Hopson and Sill grew up together as best friends. They were about the same age.

As a magistrate Sill married David Hopson and Martha Hill. They were the parents of John, Earl and Harrison Hopson.

Closing Thoughts

The wind still sings on the hills of Dogwood Flats and dips low through briars and brambles searching for the old fields and mountain meadows that once was its playground.

The tinkling of cow bells have ceased. Woodlands have slowly crept downward until their invasions are everywhere, swallowing up the old fields and cow pastures where in the long ago days of yester-year their crazy quilt patterns spread in every direction, even to the very tops of the mountains.

Like old soldiers who have lost the battle, old orchards have also yielded to the passage of time with no one to prune and keep them. The encroaching forest, shutting out the sun rays have strangled the life from their twisted trunks.

The hands that planted and cared for them have long since ceased from their labors and like a shade drawn over a window to close out the lightening flashes on a stormy night, so the sun drops behind Lonnie's Knob and twilight draws its soft curtain over a lost world and closes out the flashes of memory that sometimes are so bright they are almost startling in their intensity.

And a night bird, whose identity is still unknown to me, calls in a lonely voice from somewhere in the surrounding hills, like an echo from my childhood when I almost suffocated beneath the covers of my bed when I heard its ghostly voice, believing it to be the voice of one of the "hants" the old folks talked about.

I close my door to shut out the night sounds and to say goodbye to the past and to a life style of this section that is so far behind me and yet so hauntingly near, so near that I feel something close to pain as I think of the shadowy characters I have written about.

I feel as if I have invaded a sanctum that belongs only to them. I have stepped softly while being an interloper in order to keep their memory from perishing.

Appendix A
Little Rock Creek History

George Cook's mother was Isabel Hopson, sister of the first settler on Little Rock Creek, whose name was John. Since that time there have been many John Hopsons named in honor of their forefather John Hopson.

Isabel's son's father was a Cook. I cannot find out his given name, or anything about the Cook's at that time. It was from Isabel's son that the Cook generation spread like the wild kudzu vine, popping up in unexpected places, in different communities, different counties and different states.

George, Isabel's son, was married three times and was the father of twenty one children. Nine of them sons, who married and raised families with the exception of two of his sons-William and Sylvester. Their poignant life stories are written in this book as they were told and retold by the old timers of Dogwood Flats.

The first little log church stood in the edge of the field where Isabel stood so long ago and dreamed her dreams and saw her visions.

Figure 2 Dogwood Flats residents around 1900.

Appendix B
"George Cook's Children"

1. Madeline-Born 17 Jan 1841-Died 27 Mar 1910. She married John Winters and lived in Elk Park, NC.
2. William-Born 1842-Died 27 Feb 1862. He was on his way home from the Civil War and he and a McKinney man came down with typhoid fever. He died in Morristown and is buried in Limestone Cove.
3. Judith"Judy"-Born 5 Nov 1845-Died 8 Nov 1925. She married a man named Thomas Ledford, an old war veteran. She raised no children of her own. Her only child died at birth. She raised nine little homeless children. Thomas and Judy are buried on the Fayette Cook Cemetery.
4. Mary-Born 1846. Mary was the mother of Lafayette "Fayette", Ruben, Lemuel "Lem", John "Johnny" and George. John Birchfield was Ruben's father. George's wife struck him in the head with an iron last and injured his mind. Lem Cook lost an arm in a saw mill accident. Mary is buried in the Fayette Cook Cemetery.
5. Elizabeth "Bettie"-Born 18 Jan 1848-Died 30 Jun 1911. The name Bettie has turned up in some of the old records as well as Elizabeth. Due to the fact that I have found twenty one names Elizabeth and Bettie are one and the same-Bettie being her nickname.
6. Harriet-Born 1850-Died 17 Nov 1870. Harriet died at the age of 24 on Nov 17, 1870 when her only son Samuel Flemming "Flem" Cook was two years old. He was born 10 Apr 1868. His father was Sank Young. Harriet is buried on the Fork Mountain Cemetery but her grave is lost.
7. Jane-Born 4 Apr 1852-Died 16 May 1946. Jane was the mother of three daughters-Harriet, "name sake of Jane's sister Harriet", Pollie and Celia. Harriet married Vick Hoilman. They had one son Vincent "Vince" Hoilman. Harriet's father was John Birchfield.[19] Polly married John Buchanan. Her father was a Baker. Celia died young. The words on her tombstone read like this: Celia Cook,

> Born Oct 21 1886
>
> Died June 14 1913
>
> Gone But Not Forgotten

Celia is buried above the old Jane Cook place in a field overlooking where she was raised. It was her request to be buried there.

Pollie is buried on the Fayette Cook Cemetery. Harriet is buried on the Thomas Lenore Hopson Cemetery.

8. John-Born 13 Jun 1854-Died 1 Dec 1909.
9. Gilbert-Born 9 Dec 1860-Died 24 Jul 1919. Gilbert married Nancy Whitehead. He lived at Elk Park, Avery County, NC.
10. Ruben-Born 11 Aug 1861-Died 5 Feb 1929. Ruben married Mary Winters.

---

[19] There were two John Birchfields, "Old John", Harriet Cook's and Ruben Cook's father and "Leather Mouth John. Leather Mouth John's wife was named Ida. Many said Ida gave her mother a lot of trouble over her husband-Clate Hopson.

11. Steven-Born 1 Oct 1863-Died 7 Mar 1932. Steven married Margaret Melissa "Aunt Lissie" as she was known in her later years. Lissie was the daughter of George and Levina Hopson Gardner.

12. Jim-Born 3 Dec 1865-4 May 1940. Jim married a girl by the name of Susan Sparks. Jim's son William "Taxi Driving Will" married a girl from Popular by the name of Bertha Cooper.

13. Delilah-Born 1868. She married a man named Morgan. She is buried on the Fayette Cook Cemetery.

14. Jeremiah "Jeremine". It is spelled Jeremine in some of the family records but due to the fact that George Cook named so many of his children with bible names I am inclined to believe Jeremiah was his real name and Jeremine a shorter version or nickname.

15. Jemima "Mimmie"-Born 28 Feb 1868-Died 17 Jul 1947. Mrs. Brownlow Stanley. The Stanleys moved to Georgia where they died and are buried. They had a daughter that was named Nellie who is buried on the Fayette Cook Cemetery.

16. Naomi "Omie"-Born 1871. Naomi died when her only child, a girl named Lovie was nine months old. Moses "Mose" McKinney and his wife Mary Davis McKinney adopted Lovie and raised her. Lovie married an old veteran by the name of Colbert. They had one daughter named Olla Mae "Mrs. Clyde Yelton". Mose's wife Mary was Grant Davis' sister. Mose was a brother of George Cook's wife Bettsy "or Elizabeth her correct name." She is buried on the Greene-Garland Cemetery. Lovie, Mose and Mary McKinney, Olla Mae Colbert Yelton and husband Clyde Yelton are also buried there.

17. David "Dave"-Born 14 Feb 1873-Died 24 Feb 1944. Dave married Mollie Greene, daughter of Hoie Greene and Celia Gibbs Greene. David ran a little country store on Piney Branch. The old store house has been repaired and stands on the property now owned by Marshall Bird. David and family are buried on the Phillips Cemetery.

18. Sylvester "Sill"-Born 1875. Sill died in the old Sallie Cook house where his sister Sallie "Mrs. Samuel Yelton" lived. This was before Sallie married. Her house was located on what is now known as the Riley Cook property. Sill died of the fever and is buried on the Fayette Cook Cemetery which is located at the summit of the laurel hill west of Dogwood Flats, "now known as Cook Town". He was engaged to a girl named Nora. Nora later married Jenk Greene.

19. James.

20. Sarah "Sallie"-Born 22 Mar 1878-Died 23 Jul 1935. Mrs. Samuel "Sam" Yelton. Sallie is buried on the Huey Greene Cemetery, "now known as Garland Cemetery".

21. Lannie-Lannie married a man by the name of Harrell. They lived in Tennessee. I think in the Ripshin section. Lannie had a daughter named Ebbie Harrell. Lannie is buried in Tennessee.

One of George Cook's wives was Elizabeth "Bettsy" McKinney, daughter of Dave McKinney. Bettsy was George's wife when the 1880 census was taken. They are buried on the Fayette Cook Cemetery. One of his wives was Ebbie McGee.

Appendix C
Jane's Bald on Roan Mountain

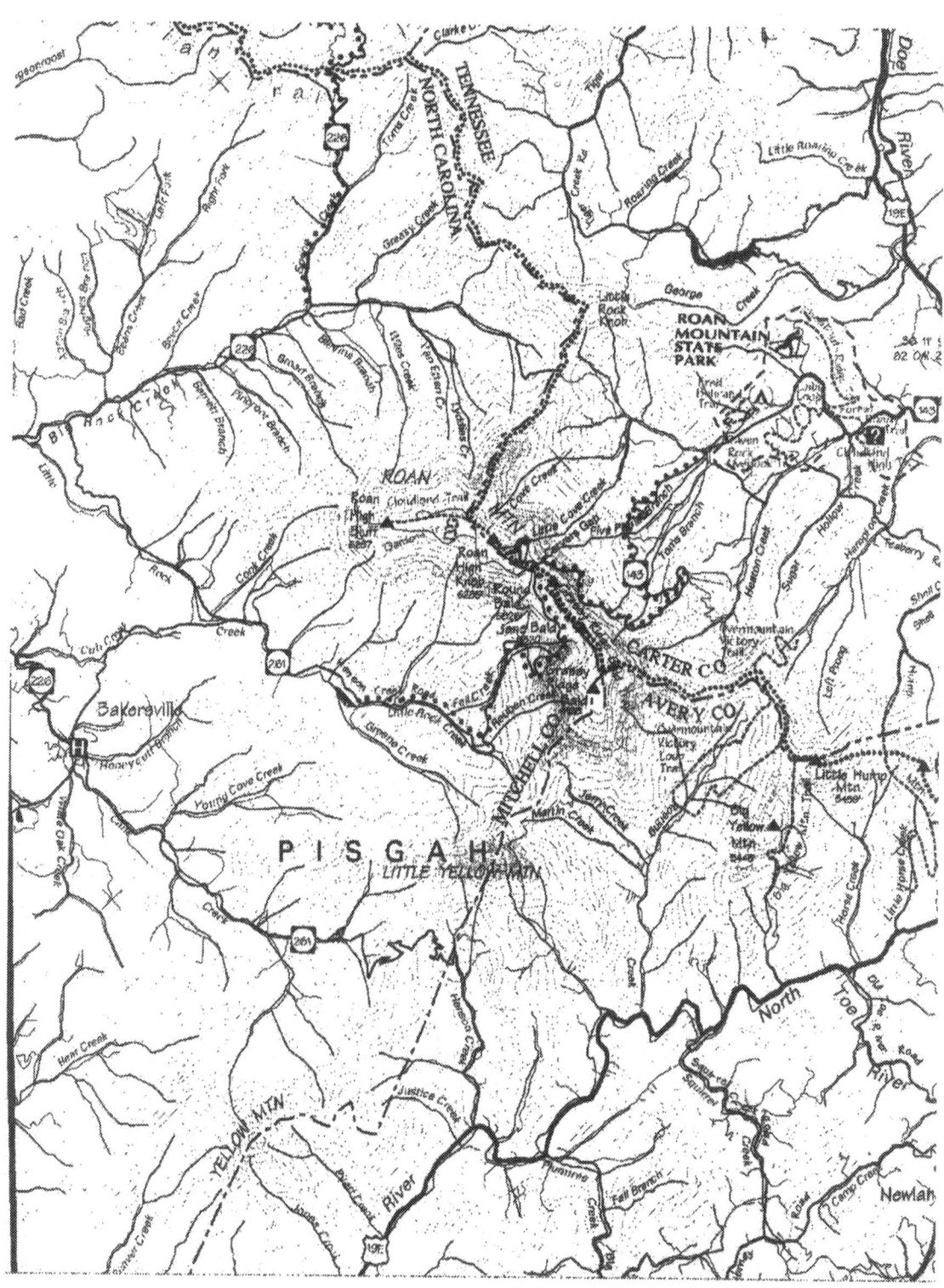

Index

A

Avery 62
Avery, Waightstill 14
Avery County 88, 98

B

Baker 98
Banner Elk 23
Birchfield, Ida 98
Birchfield, John 98
Bird, Marshall 99
Blue Ridge Mountain 2, 19, 22, 47
Borak, Rolland 36, 41, 42, 43, 47, 49, 52
Boraks 39, 40, 41
Buchanan, John 98
Burleson, Thomas 95

C

Captain Nelson 88
Colbert, Olla Mae 99
Cook, Betsy 51, 54
Cook, Celia 98
Cook, David 99
Cook, Delilah 99
Cook, Elizabeth(Bettie) 98
Cook, Fayette 88, 98
Cook, George 51, 52, 53, 54, 63, 81, 88, 93, 97, 98, 99
Cook, Gilbert 98
Cook, Granny 36, 37, 46, 49, 82, 85
Cook, Harriet 91, 92, 98, 105
Cook, Hattie 95
Cook, James 99
Cook, Jane 63, 64, 65, 91, 92, 98
Cook, Jemima 99
Cook, Jeremiah 99
Cook, Jesse 95
Cook, Jim 88, 99
Cook, John 98
Cook, Johnny 88, 98
Cook, Judy ix, 22, 80, 88, 89, 90, 91, 93, 98
Cook, Lafayette 98
Cook, Lannie 88, 99
Cook, Laura 95
Cook, Lemuel 88, 98

Cook, Lonny 42
Cook, Lovie 99
Cook, Madeline 88, 98
Cook, Mary 88, 98
Cook, Naomi(Omie) 99
Cook, Polly 92
Cook, Riley 95, 99
Cook, Ruben 88, 98
Cook, Sally (Mrs. Walter Church) 88
Cook, Samuel Flemming(Flem) 98
Cook, Sarah(Sally) 95, 99
Cook, Steven 42, 88, 99
Cook, Sylvester(Sill) 93, 95, 97, 99
Cook, William(Bill) 63, 64, 65, 97, 98
Cook, William(Curly Headed Will) 88, 99
Cook, William(Little Will) 88
Cook, William(Taxi Driving Will) 99
Cook Creek 35, 56, 63
Cook family 35, 81, 87, 94, 95
Cook Town ix, 99
Cooper, Bertha 99
Coxes Creek 12

D

Davis, Grant 99
Dogwood Flats ix, 14, 40, 42, 48, 49, 51, 52, 55, 56, 57, 62, 63, 66, 70, 74, 77, 79, 82, 88, 89, 91, 93, 95, 96, 97, 99

F

Fayette Cook Cemetery 54, 98, 99
Fork Mountain 40, 48, 53, 54, 55, 91
Fork Mountain Baptist Church 53
Fork Mountain Bluff 24, 28, 35, 56, 82, 87
Fork Mountain Cemetery 54, 98

G

Gardner, George 99
Gardner, Levina Hopson 99
Gardner, Margaret Melissa 99
Garland Cemetery 99
Glaspie Gap 11
Goff place 42
Granny Ann 42, 47
Greene, Celia Gibbs 99

Greene, Hoie 99
Greene, Jenk 99
Greene, Mollie 99
Greene-Garland Cemetery 99
Green Creek 62

H

Harrell, Ebbie 99
Hill, Martha 95
Hobson(Hopson), Isabel ix, 11, 12, 13, 14, 15,
    16, 17, 18, 19, 20, 24, 25, 26, 27, 28, 31,
    32, 33, 34, 35, 36, 37, 41, 42, 43, 44, 45,
    46, 47, 48, 49, 50, 51, 52, 53, 55, 56, 57,
    91, 97
Hobson(Hopson), John 1, 2, 3, 4, 5, 6, 7, 8, 11,
    12, 13, 14, 15, 18, 22, 23, 24, 26, 33, 34,
    35, 41, 42, 47, 48, 49, 55, 57, 59, 60, 61,
    62, 95, 97
Hobson, Elizabeth 26
Hoilman, Vick 98
Hoilman, Vincent 98
Hopson, Baxter 22, 33
Hopson, Clate 98
Hopson, David 95
Hopson, Earl 95
Hopson, Harrison 95
Hopson, John 23, 33, 62, 95, 97
Hopson, Mark 22, 23
Hopson, Mose 22, 23
Hopson, Mrs. Baxter (Nellie) 22
Hopson, Thomas Nora 33
Huey Greene Cemetery 99

I

Iron Mountain 12
Isabel, Grandmother 91

J

J.S. ix, 14, 18, 19

L

Ledford, Mrs. Hobert (Bessie) 23
Ledford, Thomas 42, 98
Lick Ridge 61
Limestone Cove, Tennessee 80, 81, 98
Little Rock Creek 6, 14, 23, 33, 53, 54, 59, 62,
    63, 80, 83, 85, 87, 88, 97, 105
Lizzie Beth 36, 37, 45, 46, 47, 48, 50

Lonnie's Knob 66, 96

M

McGee, Ebbie 54, 99
McKinney 80, 98
McKinney, Dave 54, 99
McKinney, Elizabeth (Betsy) 54, 99
McKinney, Mary Davis 99
McKinney, Moses 54, 99
McKinney Cove 61
Morgan 99

N

Nora 93, 94, 95, 99

P

Phillips Cemetery 99
Presswood place 63
Pumpkin Patch Mountain 1, 2, 28, 57, 79

R

Ripshin, Tennessee 88, 89, 91
Roan Mountain 11, 28, 57, 62, 79, 89, 91, 94,
    100
Roan Valley 14, 63, 90, 91

S

Sparks, Susan 99
Spruce Pine 11
Stanley, Brownlow 99
Stanley, Nellie 99

T

Tennessee 12, 66, 80, 81, 88, 89, 99
The Jane Bald 88, 91
The Wild Cat Rock 56
Thomas Lenore Hopson Cemetery 98
Toe 1, 20
Toe River 48
Toe River Valley vii

W

Whitehead, Nancy 98
Wilkes County 2
Winters, John 98
Winters, Mary 98

Y

Yelton, Clyde 99
Yelton, Samuel 99
Young, Sank 98

About the Author

Elsie Cook Yelton is the daughter of Samuel Fleming Cook and the granddaughter of Harriet Cook. She has spent her life in the area of Little Rock Creek within the original boundaries of the Cook settlement. She has made recording family history, stories and recollections a life long project. Without her all this information would have been lost.

A poem I found among her notes sums her life and thoughts up as follows:

> The little old lady said, "Gee!"
> I may live to one hundred and three,
> So, I'll spend my time
> by writing and rhyme
> and that will be comfort to me.